Constance Briscoe

Beyond Ugly

HODDER &
STOUGHTON

This is a work of fact. Nevertheless, some names of people and places have been
changed to protect the privacy of the individuals concerned.

Copyright © 2007 by Constance Briscoe

First published in Great Britain in 2007 by Hodder & Stoughton
A division of Hodder Headline

The right of Constance Briscoe to be identified as the Author
of the Work has been asserted by her in accordance with
the Copyright, Designs and Patents Act 1988.

A Hodder & Stoughton Book

1

A CIP catalogue record for this title
is available from the British Library

ISBN 978 0 340 93323 7 (hb)
978 0 340 93324 4 (tpb)

Typeset in Sabon by Hewer Text UK Ltd, Edinburgh
Printed and bound by Clays Ltd, St Ives plc

Hodder Headline's policy is to use papers that are natural, renewable
and recyclable products and made from wood grown in sustainable forests.
The logging and manufacturing processes are expected to conform to the
environmental regulations of the country of origin.

Hodder & Stoughton Ltd
A division of Hodder Headline
338 Euston Road
London NW1 3BH

To Martin and Francesca

Acknowledgement

Extract from *The Prophet* by Kahlil Gibran, Chapter III, 'On Marriage'.

William Heinemann, London, 1979.

Contents

I

A Little Improvement

1979

I saw the advertisement in one of the women's magazines I'd
picked up off the newsagent's shelf, tucked away at the back of
the classifieds. There were before and after photographs of
women with big noses and droopy tits; there was even a photo
of one with no tits at all and then after surgery she was a size D
cup. I did not want a D cup – that was the least of my problems
– but I certainly would like a nicer nose and my mouth could do
with some improvement. If the doctor could really perform
magic, he could remove the two large scars down the left hand
side of my face.

'You gonna pay for that?' asked the newsagent. He was
staring at me. He could see I was ugly.

'What?' I replied.

'That magazine, would you like to pay for it or would you
like to read it first?'

'Leave her alone,' said a lady on my right. 'She's got every
right to look at the magazine to see if she wants to buy it. I do it
every time I come into this shop. Go on love don't mind him,
you have a butchers.'

She was using Londoners' rhyming slang – butcher's hook,
look. Whilst they were involved in oral combat I wrote the
number of the Harley Street Clinic on the back of my hand and
put the magazine back. I didn't have enough money to buy it.

'Thank you very much,' I said, 'but I don't think I'll buy it.'

The newsagent scowled at me. I walked out on to the
Walworth Road, near the Elephant and Castle in south Lon-

don. At the nearest phone box I dialled the clinic's number. When the phone was answered I pushed my money in the coin slot.

'Good morning,' said a rather posh woman's voice. She did not come from the Elephant. 'This is the Harley Street Cosmetic Clinic, how may we help you?'

'I would like some surgery, please.'

'What is your specification?'

'What's my what?'

'What are you interested in?'

'Oh, I would like my nose done and my mouth and the scars on my face and . . .'

'Just a moment,' she said.

I pushed more money into the phone and found I was talking to another well-spoken receptionist.

'How may I help you?' she said.

'I would like some cosmetic surgery.'

'How old are you?'

'I am old enough and I've saved up some money.'

'Nevertheless, I have to ask, do you require finance?'

'What do you mean?'

'Do you require a loan?'

'No I don't. I've saved up some money.'

'And what is it that you are interested in?'

'Well, there is quite a lot I would like done.'

'You require cosmetic surgery, but for what reason?'

'Because I'm ugly, ugly, ugly.'

There was a long silence at the other end of the phone. The posh voice had suddenly dried up. It seemed an age before she spoke again.

'Why don't we make an appointment for you to come in and see Mr Anthony? There is a fifty pounds consultation fee.'

'That's OK,' I said. I had saved much more than that.

'How would Thursday of next week at 6.30pm suit you?'

'That is fine,' I said.

'I take it you have our address. Harley Street runs north from Cavendish Square, which is at the back of the John Lewis department store on Oxford Street.'

Harley Street was where all the famous doctors had their consulting rooms. I was going right to the top. I put the phone down, happy that one day soon I would no longer be ugly.

Thursday did not come quickly enough for me. Every day I looked in the mirror at my nose and my mouth; there they were staring back at me. My nose certainly could do with cutting down and the same went for my mouth. Every time I looked at them I remembered the incident with my mother and stepfather when they had refused to buy my school photograph.

'You is ugly,' Eastman had said. Now, years later, I would have the opportunity to put that right. The scars on my cheek could not be seen in the mirror unless I turned my face slightly to the right. They had faded over the years, but they were still there. They looked like a train track going across and down my face.

I counted the numbers along Harley Street. The even numbers were on one side and the odd numbers on the other. It was a road that went on for ever. Eventually I found the right one. It was a rather grand house; it didn't look like a clinic at all. As I paused by the front door, I had a slight touch of nerves. What if I was too ugly and they told me to go away? What if my nose and my mouth were beyond help? I would be stuck for ever with a face I had not chosen and did not want.

I walked past the door once and tried to peep in. I saw only a large wooden desk facing the street. I turned around and went back; this time when I got to the door I pretended to search my bag for something, anything to give me another opportunity to have a good look. I could not see the person at the desk at all. There were about seven or eight people in front of the desk in a queue. Men, women and some children between the ages of ten and fourteen. Beyond the queue going upstairs was a wide staircase; the banisters and steps were painted in a glossy white paint and a bright multi-coloured carpet ran up the middle. It looked like something out of a Hollywood film.

The queue gave me comfort that at least I was not alone. I went through the doors and joined it. No sooner had I done so, than others came and stood behind me. Waiting for my turn in the ugly queue, I held my bag with both my hands down in front of me. Because I was so nervous, I swayed from left to right trying to avoid the gaze of those who might be wondering why I needed cosmetic surgery. To my left was a huge waiting room with a beautiful ornate marble fireplace. The fire blazed in it, giving a warm glow. In the centre of the room was a large glass coffee table piled high with magazines of beautiful people in beautiful homes. There were lots of editions of *Vogue*. There were chairs all around the edge of the room, maybe twenty or even as many as thirty and a huge sofa chair below the window. They were all occupied and there were even people standing between the chairs. They were mostly women, but there was a smattering of men. The women had magazines of beautiful people in their hands. No one was talking to anyone else. They seemed anxious not to acknowledge that other people were in the room. Occasionally a mother would hush her children as if they were in church. Some of the children rolled around on the floor out of boredom and their mothers did not know what to do. As the queue moved up, the receptionist directed each person in turn to the waiting room on the right. When my turn came I said, 'I have an appointment with Mr Anthony at six thirty.'

'Ah, yes,' she said ticking me off the appointments' sheet. 'Please take a seat and Mr Anthony will see you shortly.'

I walked into the waiting room with all the others who had gone before me and stood in the far corner to the left of the huge fireplace. Looking round the room, I noticed everyone looked as nervous as I was. The magazines on the table cried out to be looked at, so like the others I picked one up as a welcome distraction. All the models with their perfect noses and nice mouths depressed me, so I replaced it.

The waiting room was used by several cosmetic surgeons, each of whom had a clinic in a different room in the building. From time to time a nurse or sometimes a doctor would come and call out a name. On the dot of 6.30 Mr Anthony came to the waiting room and called 'Miss Briscoe'. I stood up quickly, gathered my handbag and walked towards him. He was a very tall man of Mediterranean or possibly Middle Eastern appearance. His skin was dark olive and he had pale grey-blue eyes and tight curly black hair. His broad shoulders filled his suit perfectly and when he shook my hand I knew at once he was the surgeon. His handshake was soft and gentle; it was like putting my hand between sheets of the finest silk.

'Do come with me,' he said in a cut-glass accent, letting go of my hand and walking back beyond the stairs to a room at the rear of the building. As we entered through the dust green door, a nurse was waiting with a pad of paper. The doctor pointed a long graceful finger towards the seat and I sat down, letting my coat slip off my shoulders. He sat in front of me with the desk between us.

'What can I do for you, Miss Briscoe?'

'I would like to have a nose job and I would like my mouth done and I would like to have . . .'

'Hold on a minute,' said Mr Anthony. 'Let's just take this slowly, Miss Briscoe, and start at the beginning. Now, what is your name?'

'My name is Constance Briscoe.'

'And, Constance Briscoe, what is your full address?'

'Is my address important?'

'No, it is not important, but we need an address where we can contact you.'

'Well I have a temporary address at the moment and I'm about to go and live in Newcastle.'

'Well we don't need to get too technical. Why don't you give me an address where we can contact you.'

'You can usually get me at my father's address.'

'And what is that?'

'It is 215 Camberwell New Road.'

'Well, there we are. That was not too difficult was it?'

'No sir, I mean doctor.'

'Now Constance, how old are you?'

'I'm old enough, sir.'

'And what are you old enough for?'

'Well, for surgery, sir. I'm old enough to give my consent to be operated upon.'

'And how old is that Constance?'

'I'm over eighteen, sir.'

'Well, what about a date of birth?'

'Well, I'm over eighteen so that makes me an adult, sir, and so there is no problem with the operation.'

'I've got an idea, Constance. Why don't I give you this form and you can fill it out yourself. You need to know that the form will help me help you. Do you understand?'

'Yes, doctor.'

'And no one is saying that you cannot give consent if you are old enough.'

'I am old enough, sir.'

'Good, then there is no problem with you providing your date of birth, is there? Just there where it says name and address and just below that date of birth and occupation.'

Things were not going well. I had hoped to get off to a better start, but I had got myself worked up for no reason at all. It would be so bad if the doctor said that I had to remain like I was for the rest of my life. I did not wish to remain ugly.

Look at you, I thought as I filled out the form, 'You is ugly, ugly, ugly.' I remembered my mother asking where I had got my nose from – 'You have not got it from my side of the family.' Mr Anthony waited patiently for me to fill out the form; not another word was spoken as he wove his silken fingers together.

By this time I was having difficulty seeing the form, which

was only about twelve inches from my face. The tears welled up behind my eyes and they were waiting to fall; when I tried to stop them it just got worse. Large blobs ran down my face and fell splat bang onto my form. My writing became blurred and the form got soggy.

'I thought things were just too good to be true,' said the doctor as I used the side of my right hand in a swiping motion to remove the tears from the page. Unfortunately, I simply smudged it in three wide strokes that looked like blue rainbows.

'I'm sorry,' I said, as I tried to blow on the paper to assist with the drying of both the ink and the form.

'That's it!' said the doctor. 'You just carry on. You did not want to fill the form out in the first place. Now that I have insisted, you have deliberately set about sabotaging it, and why? Just because you did not want to give your age or your date of birth!'

'Oh no, doctor,' I said, 'you've got it all wrong, I would never do that.' I looked up at the doctor and at the same time my nose started to run. Now I'll never get my operation, I thought. He was laughing. He found it funny. He was not serious at all. Then suddenly I started to laugh as well and we both fell about.

'Why don't you tell me about that nose job,' he roared over my laughter, 'but first I think the nurse had better get you some tissues.'

The nurse disapprovingly slapped a tissue in my hand and the box of tissues on the desk in front of me. The doctor stretched out his arm and took hold of the top left hand corner of the form.

'I think I know what we'll do with that, nurse,' he said in a rather superior voice.

She had taken her seat behind me and as I turned to my left to look at her, she appeared round the right side of me with a wastepaper bin. The doctor dropped the sodden form in the bin and then took a bacterial wipe from his desk to clean his hands.

'Now,' he said, still laughing, 'shall we start again?'

I was more relaxed now since the doctor had not really got cross with me and the nurse was doing her best to be unobtrusive. Tearing another form from the pad the doctor removed a silver pen from his top jacket pocket and said 'We'll start at the top. Right young lady, name, Constance Briscoe, address, we have that, age, over eighteen, thank you, and date of birth?'

'18.5.1957.'

'Thank you, that means you are twenty-two now, Constance. What is your occupation?'

'I am a student.'

'And what do you study?'

'I study all sorts, but I'm going to be a lawyer.'

'Are you, just!'

'Yes.'

'Oh well, I had better be careful with what I say. Now what exactly do you want, student lawyer?'

'I would like to have my face done doctor.'

'Well that does not tell me a great deal. What is it about your face that you would like to improve?'

'Well, my nose for a start, my mouth and . . .'

'And I think we'll just concentrate on those two aspects first. Shall we start with your mouth? It seems a perfectly acceptable mouth and the same goes for your nose. Now, nurse, mirror please. Constance can you just turn to face me and relax.'

The doctor got up from his chair and pulled his jacket down and as I watched him he went over to the sink and squeezed some disinfectant onto his hands, rubbing them together vigorously under a running tap. When he had finished he used his elbows and in a sideways movement managed to turn off the running water by sliding the horizontal taps from the side of the sink so that they both met in the middle. Shaking drops from his hands, the doctor pulled a green paper hand towel from the stack at the side of the sink and dried his hands.

'Now Constance,' he said. 'Tell me what it is that you would like to achieve?'

Mr Anthony came and perched in front of me on the side of the desk.

'Look up. That's it. Now, let me see.'

Placing his hand under my chin the doctor tilted my head backwards.

'And to the left,' he said. I moved my head to the left. 'Yes, I see. Now turn to the right.'

For a few moments I wondered what the doctor was looking at. It simply could not take that long to look at a nose. I could see quite enough in two seconds flat.

'Nurse,' he said. The nurse was ready with a Kodak instant polaroid camera.

'Would you like me to switch it on?' she said.

'Yes, I'll wait until it warms up.'

I was beginning to regret this. The doctor had been looking at my nose for what seemed ages and now he wanted to take a photograph of it, as though it was the kind of nose that did not come along too often. The camera flash made me jump.

'Turn to face me!' Snap went the camera. 'And the other way, thank you.' Snap. 'There's a bit of flare.'

As each picture was taken the doctor pressed a button and the picture shot out of the bottom of the camera. He passed it to the nurse, who blew on the photograph twice before she placed it on the desk in what became a line of pictures. After the final photo was lined up, nurse went to the sink to wash her hands and the doctor went back round to his side of the desk. Sitting down he looked from one photograph to the next and then back to the first photograph.

'There is definitely some flare there,' he said. 'We can certainly improve that.'

'What is flare?' I asked. I did not know that I had a nose with flare.

'Look,' he said turning the first photo round so that I could see it the right way up. 'See the nostrils. Do you see how they give way?'

'No,' I said.

Taking a pen the doctor drew two vertical lines on the photograph from the bridge of the nose to the nostril and then repeated the same exercise horizontally placing a cross at the extremities of each nostril.

'We could take that in,' he said, making diagonal cuts at the base of each nostril. 'And here,' planting a large red cross on the bridge of my nose, 'we can make this more aesthetically pleasing.'

'How would you do that?'

'We would break this bone here.' The doctor pointed to the bridge of my nose. 'And re-shape it here,' pointing to the bottom.

'Would it make my nose look better?'

'Yes, if you think the operation is necessary, we could certainly improve its appearance.'

'Would all of that hurt doctor?'

'No. You might be a bit sore, but we use what is called twilight surgery.'

'What's twilight surgery?'

'It's a feeling or perhaps a sensation of not being asleep and yet not being awake – it's a twilight period.'

Looking at the photographs, it was there for all to see: the flare, the ugliness of my nose.

'And, doctor, what about my mouth, can you do anything about that?'

'What do you want to achieve?'

'Well, my lips are not very nice, doctor.'

'Constance, you have to live with yourself. You tell me what is not very nice about your lips. Just one minute, nurse.'

She obviously knew the routine, because she simply passed a mirror to the doctor, who held it up in front of me.

'Now, Constance, tell me what you see.'

'I'd rather not look, doctor. I know what's wrong.'

'Tell me then,' said the doctor, turning the mirror over and placing it glass down on the desk behind him.

'Well, my lips are like rubber. They stick out and my mother said they are too big and I did not get them from her side of the family.'

'Oh, did she really? When did she say that?'

'A long time ago.'

'Are you sure that you want surgery, Constance? You should think about it first and then, if you really are adamant that you wish to have the operation, we can always talk again.'

'I am certain, doctor.'

'Very well, nurse,' said the doctor.

The Polaroid was placed in his hand and again three photographs were taken.

'It's a classic teapot,' he said. 'Look at the lip, especially the bottom one. Just under the lip you can see how it protrudes so as to give the appearance of the spout of a teapot. Is this something that bothers you?'

'Yes, it is.'

'And how long has it bothered you?'

'Oh doctor, for as long as I can remember and probably even longer than that.'

'Well we can improve the appearance, but you must understand that this is cosmetic surgery and therefore you should not expect any drastic alterations. Cosmetic surgery is just that, cosmetic.'

'And how much is all of this going to cost, doctor?'

'I don't discuss money, but you will be informed by my personal assistant. If you wish to have the treatment, just pay the deposit and we will book the rest.'

'How long will it all take to get me looking normal?'

'It really is not a case of getting you to look normal, because you are already normal. It is more a question of getting you to accept your appearance, which, if you want my honest opinion, is perfectly acceptable.'

'Can I have a photo of myself doctor? It's just that I have never seen myself close up.'

'We have a policy, I'm afraid, of not handing out before and after photographs, but if you want you can always take some photographs when you get home as a keepsake.'

The doctor took some more details about my medical history and then gave me a consent form to sign.

'Oh,' he said, 'there is just one other matter I should mention. Some people of afro-caribbean origin get what is called a keloid scar, which means that the scar site is left raised with a slightly shiny appearance. It can be unsightly, but we do not know how your skin will react until the healing process begins.'

'Well, now that you have mentioned it, doctor, what about the scars on my face? Can anything be done about those?'

'I think we should concentrate on what you think are the more obvious aesthetically displeasing aspects of your presentation and maybe re-visit the scars on a later occasion.'

Nurse did the tidying up and the doctor again washed his hands.

'Constance, I have all sorts of patients who visit me. Some I refuse to operate on, because I know just from talking to them that they will never be happy with the outcome of cosmetic surgery. They are just trouble. In your case, you are very young to be as determined as you are for these cosmetic changes. Why not consider the options and maybe in a couple of years' time, when your face is more mature, come back and we can talk again. Will you think about it?'

'No, doctor.'

'Why not? It is a very serious step to take.'

'I know doctor, but I have thought about it and I would like the operation as soon as possible and if it is possible I would like something done about my scars.'

'What caused them?'

'It was a plane, doctor, the wing caught me across the face.'

'Oh!' said the doctor, taking a closer look at my face. 'Are you sure it was a plane?'

'Yes.'

'The wing, you say?'

'The left wing.'

'And how did you get the second scar?'

'The plane turned and came at me again and that's when I got the second scar.'

The doctor examined my face intently.

'Constance, there is just one thing that I would like to ask and please do not take it the wrong way.'

'Sure,' I said.

'Have you ever seen a psychiatrist?'

'No, do I need to see one, doctor?'

'You tell me.'

'No, I'm fine, doctor.'

'Who was steering the plane at the time it crashed into the side of your face?'

'My mother.'

The doctor stopped examining my scar and looked me in the face; he was trying to see if I was kidding.

'And why do you think she did that?'

'She does not like me very much, doctor.'

I got the impression that the doctor was looking into my eyes to detect any sign of madness.

'And how long have you had the scars, Constance?'

'Oh, since I was about twelve, I think.'

'I think that we will have to look at the scars with a little more care, because they are on your face and we have to be sure that they can be improved. Will you leave that one with me and we will look at it again?'

'Yes.'

'Is there anything else that you would wish to raise before we draw the meeting to a close?'

'Well, you mentioned that I might get keloid scarring. I don't think I will get it, so that is OK.'

'And what do you base that opinion on, Constance?'

'I had an operation years ago and it did not leave any raised scars.'

'Where did you have that operation?'

'In St Thomas's.'

'Where on your body?'

'On my tits.'

'And this was when, you say?'

'Oh, I was fourteen.'

'That is indeed very good news that you did not get keloid scarring, but would you mind showing me the scarring just so I can check.'

'Here,' I said pointing to my left breast in a sweeping motion across the top, 'and here again' moving to my right breast in a circular movement across the top of the breast from left to right, 'and here down the side of my right breast.' The doctor got out his pen again and opened my file.

'I'll just make a few notes if you don't mind,' he said, drawing a crude pair of tits and criss-crossing them with horizontal and vertical strokes.

'May I . . . do you think that I could see the area you have referred to?'

He was very hesitant in case I took offence. I did not mind showing him my tits – at least they looked better than my face.

'Yeah, sure.'

I unbuttoned my black C&A jumper and undid the top three buttons on my blouse and pulled the blouse open. I had on my bra from East Street market, thank goodness. It was white and had very beautiful pale lilac buds with tiny perforations around the edge. I had only bought it on the spur of the moment. The doctor just looked at my breasts from a distance and thanked me. As I did up my blouse, he went back round to his side of the desk, sat down again and opened my file.

'How did that happen?'

'My mother,' I said.

'And what did she do?'

'Well she used to pinch my buds and the doctors had to operate to get the lumps out.'

The doctor did not look up as he wrote his notes. He was suddenly very serious.

'You don't still live with your mother?'

'No, I haven't for years.'

He looked relieved.

'Do you have any other scars?'

'Yes I do.' I rested my right hand on the desk and pointed to a circular scar on the back of it.

'See,' I said, 'no keloid scarring.'

The doctor glanced over at the back of my hand and using the index finger of his left hand brushed over the scar.

'Yes, it does suggest that you heal very well. Was that caused by your mother?'

'Oh no, doctor, my mother did not do that; my stepfather did. My mother did this one.'

I pulled up the sleeve on my cardigan, undid the cuff button on my blouse and rolled up the sleeve. I turned my arm over on his desk so that my hand was palm side up and pointed out the scar.

'That is a vertical scar running, shall we say, five inches or thereabouts. What caused that?'

'A knife, doctor, but it has healed very well.'

'Yes, I cannot argue with that. Have you ever told any other doctors how you got these scars?'

'No, doctor, but can you sort them out?'

'No,' said the doctor, laughing again. 'Constance you must not be so impatient. I have already said that we will revisit the matter.'

For the second time the doctor closed my file and yet again he washed his hands, as the nurse sat silently behind me.

'Now, Constance, I don't think that there is anything else, but if there is please feel free to raise it.'

'No, doctor. I don't think that there is.'

'Well, it's been most interesting meeting you, Constance. You do seem very easygoing about your past.'

'Am I easygoing doctor?'

'Yes, and you make me laugh. I am sure that we will meet again and I am sure we can do something for you. Please think about whether you really want to go through with these intrusive operations. Surgery is a very big deal and you should think about it a little more, but I have a feeling that you have already decided. Is that right?'

'Yes, doctor.'

'Well, until we meet again.' He stood and offered me a silky hand.

'Constance you are not ugly, you only think you are.'

'No, doctor, you are wrong.'

'Nurse will show you out.'

I could have gone on shaking that hand for ever, but I picked up my bag and followed the nurse back to reception.

'The doctor will be in touch soon,' she said.

As I left, I glanced into the waiting room. It was overflowing with people, fat ones, thin ones, old ones, young ones. They all wanted to be beautiful. I was beautiful already. The doctor had said that. Well, almost. I was just going to have a few small adjustments to my face.

The following Tuesday I got a letter explaining that the cost of the operation for my mouth was just under a thousand pounds per lip! To have my flare removed would cost another fifteen hundred pounds! There was no mention at all about the cost of having the scar removed. The letter suggested that I might consider having just the one lip done and then on a later occasion I could have the other done. The operations and the cost could be spread over a period of years, if that was what I wanted. The doctor could book me into surgery as soon as I definitely decided to go ahead. The cost of the Harley Street consultation would be deducted from the cost of the surgery. In any event the doctor would wait to hear from me, but if there were any other questions I should not hesitate to contact him.

Sitting on my bed, I realized that I simply did not have that sort of money. I had saved up for a rainy day, but all my rainy day money would not pay for the surgery I needed. The doctor mentioned that I could take out a loan, but that would take me forever to pay off. I put my letter away. I would think about it all later. I was determined to pay the deposit if I could.

2

No Dreaming Spires

1979

In late September I took an overnight train to Newcastle Upon Tyne in the north of England, not far from the Scottish border. I travelled overnight, because it was cheaper. Here was I, a girl whose mother had said she was too stupid to go to university, on my way. I had never felt so free, so happy, but then I thought sadly of the teacher who had befriended me when I was at my lowest – Miss K. She had told me I could achieve anything I wanted. How proud she would have been of me now! I had not seen her since shortly after she lost her leg in an accident in Poland. I had offered to look after her, but she had refused, saying she would only hold me back. She was wrong. Miss K and Miss B would have got on fine.

I had applied for a single room in a students' hostel, but the bursar wrote back and told me that I would have to share a room with another student. Some first year students found it difficult to live on their own and so there was a policy of sharing. I would not have found it difficult to live on my own; I had lived on my own and virtually brought myself up for the last seven years.

The sky was almost black as the train pulled away. It was a Royal Mail train that would stop at every station to deliver and collect post, so I snuggled down to get some much needed sleep.

I had been so worried about how I would survive financially at university that I had taken time off to work and save before taking up my place. I had previously worked in a hospice in Lyndhurst Gardens, Belsize Park and now I got a job again there doing night duty as an auxiliary nurse. I was known then as Clearie or Clare; it was only later that I found out that the name on my birth certificate was Constance. At the hospice I kept my old name. Belsize Park is a leafy suburb in north London near the top of Haverstock Hill. The hospice was in a large, tall Victorian house. As I walked towards it on the first evening, I passed beautiful warm brick houses on every side and dreamt that one day I would own such a house. It was, as Miss K would say, no more than I deserved.

Part of my duty on the night shift was simply making the patients comfortable, giving them tea or coffee, filling their water jugs, turning back the beds and giving out bed pans. Sometimes I would take the patients who could walk to the toilet and, if sister and the full-time nursing staff were busy, I would be allowed to take the patients' temperature and blood pressure.

One of the jobs that I was allocated was preparing the bodies of the recently dead. Many of the patients who were at Lyndhurst Gardens were in the final stages of life. When it was apparent that a patient in a four bed ward was dying, he or she would have the curtains pulled around their bed. It might sound strange, but I always thought it was a complete pleasure to sit with someone who was close to death. When I was on duty I would hold their hand. I spoilt the ladies. I would brush their hair for them and clean their face and neck. Sometimes I washed their important other bits and put some make up on them – nothing too obvious, just something to give a bit of colour in their cheeks. It matters to look one's best. Sometimes I would give their dentures a good wash or scrub with a nail brush. I never worked on the day duty, only nights from eight in the evening to eight in the morning. A very stressful night might include two people dying. Sometimes in the summer we would lose three all in one night.

Making the dead attractive for their relatives is an art in itself. You must start as soon as life is gone. We were told by

Sister that sometimes those final touches can make the difference between a relative accepting death or storing up serious
problems for the future. A peaceful looking corpse is one the
relatives might think was happy to go, whereas one that looked
depressed and unhappy might give the opposite impression. I
could always make a lady pretty in death, but it was sometimes
more difficult to perform the same kind of magic on the
gentlemen. There were not many opportunities to tidy up
and make a dead male presentable, though a shave could help.
Luckily the men seemed not to die when I was on duty. The
only time that I can see in my mind's eye looking after a dead
man was when he had told me that his male lover would be
arriving at the hospice shortly and he wanted to look his best.
He was so ill that he was quite unable to get up out of bed even
to help himself to a drink. He wanted his hair combed with a
parting just so and clean dentures. All of his requests were met.
I said goodbye to him when I finished my shift, fully expecting
him to be there when I returned later that evening. I had gone to
his room specifically to tell him that I was off home. At first he
had not heard me, his head was turned away from me, looking
out of the window. He was so weak he could barely move his
head and his shoulders looked like a half closed umbrella with
the handle skewiff. I whispered a little louder. 'I'm off now I
just came to say "bye".' He did not even acknowledge me. His
hands were over the sheet and counterpane, which were tucked
in tight under the mattress. His arms were thin and mauve and
the veins in his hands stood proud and were pulsating madly.
'I'm off,' I said again, this time very gently covering his hand
with mine. He turned his head towards me.

'Oh Clearie, it's you,' he said. 'Please be a love and pull my
curtains.' I let go of his hand and walked round the bottom of
the bed and pulled the curtains. 'Do you think you could pull
me up the bed,' he asked. When I tried to pull him up the bed, I
couldn't. I went off to find another nursing assistant and
between the two of us we managed to pull him up on the

undersheet and then propped him against the bed rest. We plumped up the pillows and made him comfortable.

'Anything else?' I asked.

'Clearie, if you've got a moment do you think you could give me a drink?'

I poured some water into a beaker and put it to his lips. He dribbled and I put a towel under his neck to stop him getting sore. When he was finished I wiped down his face, replaced his beaker and said, 'See you later.'

'Will you?' he replied.

I thought nothing of it until I returned for duty that evening and, as Sister gave the handover reports, she said that he had died. I honestly could not understand why he would die just like that. Of course he looked ill, but not that ill. I was devastated by his death. Our lives had passed each other only briefly and yet his death affected me so badly that I could not bear to go into his room. When I eventually did, I was convinced that he was lying on the bed asking me to fetch him his dentures and brush his hair. It must have been only two days later that someone else was booked into the room. How I resented that. My poor old patient hadn't been dead long and there was already some other pretender in his room. The night sister said I had a way with patients – sympathetic and caring. I did not feel I was that special, but I knew the patients liked me.

When I was about to go to university I arranged to go back to Lyndhurst Gardens as often as possible at the weekends. It was an opportunity to earn money to keep me during my three years. I was so used to being on my own, I could not imagine making that many friends in Newcastle.

The Royal Mail drew into Newcastle Upon Tyne station in the early hours of the morning. I had made separate arrangements for my rocking chair and television to follow me. From the station I took a taxi with my two metal suitcases to Leazes

Terrace. It was still dark and the streets were silent. I wondered what life in this strange place would be like.

My only other visit had been for an interview for a place in the law faculty. With my three As at Advanced level I felt pretty confident of getting in. One of the professors wanted to know why I had chosen to come all the way to Newcastle, when I could have stayed nearer to home. I paused to think what sort of answer they wanted and, as I could not think what it might be, I simply told the truth.

'I want to get as far away from my mother as I can and I don't want to go back to her as long as I am here.'

The professors were a little taken aback. After a whispered conversation they called a third teacher, a Mr Stevenson, to join the interview. He was a round sort of chap, who was clearly a member of the aristocracy or as near as damn it. He kept saying 'There, there' and 'What' and then he mentioned fine wine and called me a good fellow. At the end of the interview he asked me why I thought they should take me. Again I had no answer, so I said 'Because I will take you.' They all started to laugh and I thought that I had blown the interview, but then Professor Clark said: 'Promise me, Constance, that if we offer you a place you will accept.' I said, 'Of course I will' and Professor Elliot said, 'I can tell you now we intend to offer you a place.' I was very happy about that so I said, 'I can tell you now I intend to accept.'

Leazes Terrace was not exactly the dreaming spires. It was one of a number of seven storey blocks built in brute concrete. I had to get the porter out of bed, but he was remarkably good tempered, asking me how I liked travelling at night. He suggested that I leave my cases outside his office door, while he showed me to my room. Once I knew where it was I could take my time getting my stuff up there. My room was on the third floor of the mixed student block. It was nice enough, but I really did not know how to share a room with another person and in truth I had no idea how to be a student. The room seemed quite small for two people. My bed was to the left as you entered and the other bed was to the right. Immediately in front of my bed was a decent sized desk and at the bottom of the bed a small wardrobe. It was fine enough. On each landing was a washroom, bathroom and toilet with a huge concrete eating area in the basement. There were dozens of fridges, tables, sinks and cookers stretching from one end of the building to the other. It was very clean and orderly. The cookers were spotless and the fridges clean and fresh. The porter offered me a tour of the building and when I accepted gave me a plan and left me to get on with it.

After my night journey, I was exhausted. I fell onto the bed and could not remember a thing until the next morning. The bed was tiny: if you turned round in a hurry you might fall off the end. I had never slept in such a tiny bed and the mattress was paper thin. I had left a perfectly good bed back in London to sleep in a tiny bed with a mattress that was paper thin! When I finally awoke, my belongings were waiting to be put away in my allocated wardrobe and my desk. The room was pale green, like the walls of the hospitals I had worked at over the years. I looked out of the window. A grim sea of concrete greeted me.

I was told that my room mate, Louise, was a mature student, an ex social worker. I hadn't really thought about it, but I was probably a mature student too, as I had worked before I came up. I wondered what it would be like to share a room with another person, whom I did not know apart from her name. Did she know that I was black? Would it make any difference? Probably not if she was a social worker. I had already decided not to like her anyway, simply because I had to share the room with her. Maybe I wasn't so mature! When Louise turned up, I found that we did have something in common. Like me, she had a clear vision of what she wanted to do and how she intended to achieve it. We soon found a way of living together.

Freshers' Week was due to begin on Monday. I had no idea what this involved apart from the fact that the brochure said it was not to be missed. Students from all over the country would descend on their chosen university and enjoy three days of socialising. All the freshman students would meet at an array of clubs and future events in the students' union. When Freshers' Week started, I had never seen so many people congregate with the sole purpose of having a good time. Newcastle was full of clubs, pubs and violence, but the Geordies were so friendly that they took the chill away from the northern icy temperatures. I was informed by the ticket inspector on the way up that a Geordie could hold his drink. I came to appreciate that this was not always true.

Meeting so many different people from so many different backgrounds during Freshers' Week made me feel sad. Everyone appeared to have had a straightforward life. Most of the students had come direct from school and home. Some got homesick. Even amongst the mature students very few had taken time off simply because they needed to earn money. Some had been travelling, others started on a job and then decided they would like a degree and others still had delayed coming because they wanted to have babies. No one had taken time off because of their family circumstances, as I had. Everyone seemed to have normal families. When I was asked why I'd taken time out, I could hardly say that my mother had refused to sign my grant application form. Anyway, that was not strictly true. She had torn it up like confetti and thrown it in the air. I could hardly say that I'd had to earn the right to get a grant on my own account and so had to work for several years to qualify. I did not want anyone feeling sorry for me, or doing me special favours, so the less everyone knew about my background the better.

At Freshers' Week it seemed everyone had come up specifically to get drunk. Alcoholic drink had never been on my agenda – the highest I had ever aspired to was Coke. It had never crossed my mind to drink wine or beer, never mind vodka and cider. The students seemed quite happy to mix them and were surprised when I was offered alcohol and refused.

'Why? Are you a Muslim?'

'Muslim has nothing to do with it.'

'Well, are you religious?'

I thought I was, but that too had nothing to do with it – I did not drink because I did not drink. After the first astonished reaction, people left me alone. No one made a big deal out of it.

The first year law students were invited to meet one another and the professors. This apparently was a privilege bestowed every year on the new recruits. I turned up at the appointed time in the reception room, where there was a table laid out with an assortment of refreshments: red and white wine, tea, coffee, orange juice, biscuits and cheese. I did not know that you could get so many different types of cheese. There was yellow cheese and a sort of orange cheese, cheese with blue veins, and then there was a flat round cheese with what appeared to be a white leather skin on top. Someone said it was brie. I was sure the cheese with blue veins was mouldy because it smelt so bad, but when we were invited to help ourselves most of the students started piling the mouldy cheese onto their plates together with a large helping of the cheese with the leather skin. There was another cheese that had a thick crusty edge all the way around the outside; it reminded me of the back of my mother's heels. It did not smell that nice and again it appeared to have blue mould all over the inside. Maybe someone had stabbed the cheese with a fountain pen and then squeezed the ink deep into the heart of the cheese which had then bled. The smell and appearance did not put off anyone except me. I stuck to what I was familiar with, cheddar cheese and cream cracker biscuits.

I went up to one girl who was quite tall, about five feet eight with shoulder length hair. She had very red cheeks. She wore a grey cardigan/coat that came down to her mid thigh. She seemed sophisticated. I told her my name and as she looked down at me she burped loudly. The girl next to her, who turned out to be called Pauline Moulder, looked round in surprise. The tall girl burped again, this time rather louder and longer. It was like a string of bubbles going through a narrow wet tunnel. We all started to laugh and the tall girl was in hysterics bent double. The other students looked horrified. The first year students were misbehaving. We managed to introduce ourselves. She was Jo. She spoke quite posh and seemed quite jolly, though that might just have been the drink. The evening had hardly started and already she had taken too much.

The professors swept in and immediately the atmosphere changed. The third year students were very polite, almost humble. I decided to try some small talk with the professor. He was tall and distinguished, rather like a grey-haired George Clooney.

'How are you finding Newcastle?' he asked.

'Oh,' I said, 'it's too cold and my bedroom is this big.' I stretched out my arms. 'There is not enough room to swing a cat.'

'Why would you want to swing a cat?'

'I don't want to swing a cat,' I said.

'And why would you want to walk around the room with your arms outstretched?'

'I don't,' I said.

'Well, if you don't want to swing a cat and you don't want to walk around the room with your arms outstretched, then the room must be ideal!'

I was to realise this was his teaching method – to make you question every proposition. Pauline sent over a young man called J to give me moral support. He chatted to the professor. J was pretty good-looking, too, in his heavy leather jacket and Doc Marten's boots. He made a nice contrast to the suave professor. J spoke in a slight cockney accent, with posh over-tones. He had probably been privately educated. I suddenly thought that Miss K would have liked J; I think she would have said that the young gentleman had potential.

Other students gravitated towards us. Professor Ellie, as

some of us came to call him, was a big name in academic law. He was an expert in the law of evidence. His looks and brains and sense of humour proved a magnet for all of us. He noticed I did not have a drink and asked if I would like one. I told him that I did not drink and he looked astonished.

'You,' he said, 'Miss Briscoe, have chosen to spend three years reading law, yet you tell me that you do not drink. Do you see any inconsistency in those two statements?'

'No,' I said, 'I don't think so.'

'Then I shall ask you again at the end of three years.'

As Prof. Ellie moved on to meet and greet other people, I walked with J back to a seat in the bay window and joined Pauline and Jo.

Jo's cheeks were red, apple red and it was obvious to those of us in the window seats that the third year students were not happy with us at all.

I sat with what seemed to have become our group, drinking orange juice. I introduced myself.

'I'm Constance,' I said. 'Constance Briscoe, and I'm from London.' The others introduced themselves. Jo was a local girl, she lived in Newcastle with her parents. Newcastle was not her first university. She had apparently studied medicine at Oxford, but she was such a wild child that she was invited to leave the university and to consider reapplying when she was older and more equipped to cope with life as an undergraduate. She proved to be clever, very clever and quite the most articulate person that I had ever met. She was also very kind and sincere. You could rely on Jo. She became a good friend of mine.

Pauline was a good laugh. She was older than the rest of us, nearly thirty. She had previously worked on a newspaper and she had a husband and two children. She had always wanted to study law. She too was clever, but not in Jo's league. She was quite rough-spoken and always had a fag in her hand. Always dressed in jeans, she was quite small, like me, and plump but not tubby. Her hair was black and cut in the equivalent of a short back and sides. She had small features and the darkness of her hair gave her an almost Spanish look. She was quite attractive, but seemed unaware of it. She also was someone you could rely on.

All of us had taken time out, even J. He looked young, though, and had that sort of 'I've never shaved' baby skin. His nose was too large for him to be really good looking. He had a centre parting and hair flopping down to the side and layered from the fringe to the back of his head. I did find him attractive. I could see some of the girls in the year above us casting 'I could fancy you' looks at him. Unfortunately he had a girlfriend back home in Welwyn Garden City and he spoke of her a bit too often and went back to see her most weekends.

Having done something before we came to university gave us a common bond that made us just a little different from those students who had come straight from school. I was happy with my new found friends. I don't think that I had ever had so many friends in my entire life. We started going to parties as a group. Pauline and Jo lived locally and J was in Leazes Terrace, though in a different house from mine. We met up easily. My old flat in 19 Sutherland Square and my mother were things of the past. I had promised myself that I would never speak again to my mother. I was sure that I would keep that promise.

Once term began we got down to work and although the classes started at 9am most days we all managed like dutiful freshers to get in on time. Our group of friends widened to about eight or ten students. The second week of term we all went to the pub. I had never been into a pub before. Everyone knew that I did not drink alcohol. I ordered lemonade in a half pint glass. Some of my group asked if I had ever been drunk.

'Of course not,' I replied.

'Never ever?'

'Never in my life.'

This reply prompted swift action and they laced my drink with vodka, but I was able to detect it straight away. On other occasions they would try gin, but again I knew what they had done. I hated all the attention. In the end I decided to order my own drinks and that put an end to it.

The term got off to a good start. I quite enjoyed my subjects, although I was now so comfortable in bed that I had some difficulty in getting up. It was not that I was not organized. I was. But the fact was, now that my bed-wetting days were behind me, there really was no reason why I could not stay in bed for ever. Life was quite orderly. I knew exactly where I had to be and what I was doing during term time. I quite enjoyed land law. Professor Clark was my hero – listening to him was always interesting, if sometimes confusing. I managed to get to grips with land law between 1285–1837. Law of Property Act 1925 was supposed to make things simpler to understand. It did not help me at all and I got confused with fee simple and fee tail, not to speak of entails and conditional fee simple. I had to admit I was completely lost for the whole term. Professor Clark said I should not worry. Most students found it difficult to start off with and it would become clearer with the passage of time. When we moved on to wills and intestacy I was on much firmer ground and settled down to become quite good at land law.

I found administrative and constitutional law rather dry subjects. We first-year students did not have any choice in what we studied: there was a set syllabus to give us a good general grounding. I was in Group B of my land law seminar and for my first piece of work I got 13 out of 20, which was not bad for a subject I struggled in. Contract and tort (which is basically wrongs against others which can lead to claims for compensation) I found easier; they were the kind of law that could crop up in everyday life. Our first lecture in contract was quite interesting. It introduced us to the function of contract in society, traced from feudal times to the beginnings of modern contract law.

Studying the law of contract reminded me about my own outstanding contract. I had to take a decision on my cosmetic surgery. I had been getting through my grant quite slowly. There was not much to spend it on. The rent for my student accommodation was deducted before I got the remainder so all I had to do was to look after myself. I also had the earnings from my work at the hospice. If I could get work there at Christmas, I could pay for the operation and just about get through next term. I decided I was definitely going to have the operation.

3
The Doctor's Dilemma

1979

Dear Mr Anthony,

Thank you for seeing me and discussing with me the pros and cons of cosmetic surgery. I have now decided that I would like to have the operation on my nose as soon as possible and delay the other operations we discussed. I enclose a £100 cheque by way of deposit and look forward to hearing from you in due course. If at all possible I would like the operation at the end of my second term. Easter is a good time for me. I have not quite decided about the other operations yet, but I have a feeling that I will probably go ahead with them. I look forward to hearing from you soon.

Constance Briscoe

It was a few days later when I got a letter from the doctor. He acknowledged my cheque and was happy to book me in for surgery, if I was sure that that was what I wanted. He had a nagging doubt about carrying out the operation and therefore before a final decision was made he would like me to see him again at Harley Street, free of charge. For some reason I got it into my head that I was just too ugly for the surgeon's knife and he wanted to let me down as gently as he possibly could. Getting to London was difficult. I was not prepared to miss any of my classes and I wanted to see Mr Anthony as soon as possible so that he could tell me face to face what he wasn't prepared to put in a letter.

I rang his number and the receptionist answered, but the

doctor was operating and could not come to the phone. I explained about the recent letter I had received and was told to leave it with her overnight and she would contact the doctor. I suggested that I travel down to London on my half study day. My fare would be significantly reduced with my student rail card and I could travel back to Newcastle on the same day. When I contacted the receptionist the next day, she informed me that the doctor would see me the following Wednesday at 3pm. That was the time that had been pencilled in, but if I arrived earlier the doctor would try to fit me in. I thanked her and she said I should have a nice day.

The next Wednesday, whilst most of the students were spending their free time in the library or at home preparing work or research, I travelled down to Kings Cross Station and then got a bus to Harley Street. The doctor saw me more or less at the agreed time. The nurse assisting him was an older woman, not the same one as the last time I was there. She introduced herself and shook my hand warmly. She had blue eyes and her facial skin seemed pulled back tightly. I wondered whether the doctor had performed magic with his silken hands on her.

'I'm glad you came, Constance,' he said extending his hand to me. My skin seemed rough against his.

'I just wanted to go through a few issues that were troubling me,' he said. 'You see, young lady, I just cannot make you out. There are some patients I see whom I refuse point blank to operate on. There are others who I know would benefit from cosmetic surgery, but are so intense and insecure that no amount of surgery will ever make them feel good about themselves. Then I have a very small category of patients that are difficult to pigeon-hole and even more difficult to predict. I am telling you this because you are an intelligent woman.'

'OK.'

'I feel I don't really know you at all. For example, which category do you belong to?'

'I don't know, doctor. I don't think I belong to one or the other.'

'That is precisely what I mean,' he said. 'Constance, tell me why you want to have cosmetic surgery.'

'Does the reason matter?'

'I think it does.'

'Well, I can give you an answer which will be acceptable to you.'

'Why don't you give me a true answer? Stop second guessing me.'

'I am ugly, doctor.'

'I disagree.'

'Well you may disagree, but beauty is in the eyes of the beholder.'

'Ah, but you see I am the beholder, not you. It is your internal picture of yourself which says you are ugly. It is not true. I am not going to tell you you are beautiful, because your own perception would refuse to believe me, but I promise you, you are not ugly. You are young and yet so determined. Ought you not to wait a few years before you finally make up your mind?'

'No, doctor, I want it done as soon as possible.'

'But why do you wish to go through all that? It can be quite traumatic and whatever I do you may feel I have not made much difference.'

'Doctor,' I said, 'I have lived with myself for years. Ever since I've known myself I've known that I was ugly and that ugliness has bothered me all my life.'

'But you are an attractive woman, Constance.'

'I know otherwise,' I said. 'I know you can improve my looks.'

'But can we really achieve your expectations, Constance? You may think you are the ugly duckling who will be turned into a swan. It doesn't work quite like that in real life. If I told you you are a swan already you wouldn't believe me.'

'You told me I had a flared nose.'

'Yes I did, but I did not tell you that you needed surgery.'

'And you told me I had a teapot mouth.'

'I said a teapot bottom lip, but I did not say you needed surgery. Constance, you have to have surgery for yourself, not because of stray phrases you have picked up from me.'

'But I am having it for me, doctor. I am not having it for anyone else. It will improve the person I am.'

'Constance, I can only work with the material I have. You are young, your skin is able and the elasticity and texture of your skin is excellent.'

'Then operate, doctor.'

'The whole point of this consultation was to find out more about you and to make sure that you are having the operation for the right reasons. I don't feel as if I have made any progress.'

'You have, doctor.'

'But I still don't know what makes you tick, Constance, or who you are.'

'Tell me about the surgery, doctor. What does it involve?'

'Rhinoplasty? In your case it involves removing some nasal bone and cartilage. Surgery is performed internally, inside the nose and that leaves no scars. In your case the operation will leave tiny scars at the base of your nose which will heal with time and eventually disappear.'

'Will it hurt doctor?'

'Well no, you will be quite sore for two to three weeks, but after that the soreness will disappear. Post operative changes will be apparent within a two to three month period, but the full effect may take as long as nine months.'

'What about the operation?' I said. 'How long does that take?'

'The surgery will be twilight or under a general anaesthetic depending on its complexity. It normally takes about an hour and you will have to stay overnight. You will have a small nose splint to maintain the early stages of healing.'

'Well, it all sounds excellent, doctor. I am looking forward to a new me.'

'You will be the same you,' said the doctor, 'but maybe you will feel a little better about yourself. Well, if you are so determined, we'll book you in for the first Wednesday after Easter. The nurse will write to you and let you know what you will need to bring with you.'

Shaking the doctor's hand, I stepped out into a clear blue sky and sharp November breeze. I almost danced down the street. I caught the bus back to King's Cross station. Sitting on the train, I could not help but smile.

Back in Newcastle I studied my face in the mirror. It was true, it did not look that bad. On the other hand, it did not look that great. I imagined my face with a better nose, a nicer mouth and no scars. In bed just before I went to sleep, I pictured an altogether prettier Constance and then I saw Miss K wagging her finger.

'Constance, you can be anything you want but you must believe in yourself.'

'I am beginning to, Miss K!'

I had trouble concentrating on my studies after that, but that was not my only problem. The other was finance. I had committed myself to paying Mr Anthony £1000. My grant money was not enough to finance my living expenses and my savings did not cover the cost of the operation. I had thought about asking the doctor if I could have a student discount, but I remembered that he had told me that cosmetic surgery does not come cheap. My plans were falling apart and they had not even begun. I contacted the hospice to see if they wanted me to work during my half term. They did. Brilliant. I had arranged to stay in a room above the hospice with one of the nurses for a small fee. The other option was to go and stay with my father in one of his houses. That would be free, but I never knew where to find him and I did not want to waste time hunting for my dad.

Over the mid term break, I managed to work seven full nights. The sister on night duty had white hair, soft and curly. She was in her mid to late fifties and was terribly pleased that she was a sister and in charge. I don't think she realised I was an old hand by now. When we had the handover report, she looked surprised to see me taking a note and then, when I went off to sort out the tea and collect the cutlery, she suddenly appeared behind me in the kitchen. I told her I was about to collect the cups and she said she would come back later. Once that was finished I got my trolley from the sluice and prepared my bedpans. Starting in the first ward I was in with the patient in the third bed, giving her a bedpan behind the curtains, when Sister appeared again.

'Oh there you are,' she said.

'Yes I am,' I said, bemused. 'Is there something you would like me to do?'

'Well no,' she said. 'You just carry on and I'll catch up with you later.'

This was becoming a game of hide and seek. I continued from room to room with my bedpans and carried on until all the patients had been seen and then I went into the sluice to clean the area and put away the final bedpans. Sister turned up again behind me.

'Oh there you are!' she said again. 'We seem to keep bumping into each other.'

I smiled, all innocence. She went off to continue dispensing drugs and I tidied the bedside tables and beds, and puffed up the pillows until each patient was settled and the side light could be turned off. I made my way into the kitchen to wash all the cutlery that was on the side. Sister appeared again, but this time she did not say anything, just washed her hands and made herself a cup of tea.

'Everyone had a bedpan, Nurse Clare?'

'Yes, Sister, all those that wanted one.'

'Have they had their nightcap?'

'Yes, Sister, and they have all been settled down for the night.'

'Do you know, Nurse Clare, I don't remember a time when I did not have to tell an auxiliary nurse what to do. You've just got on with it without any prompting at all. I'm very impressed.'

'Thank you, Sister,' I said. 'Is there anything else that you wish me to do?'

'No, Nurse. I think you deserve a cup of tea.'

I made myself a cup and then went round the dayroom to collect the old newspapers and magazines. I piled them up in the staff room for the nurses. Then we did one final check to make sure all the patients had what they required to get a good night's sleep.

Time on night duty passes very quickly, because although there is a dead period between 2 and 5 am, the whole process starts again in the morning with a round of bedpans, drinks, bedpans again and then tidying of the beds. I was exhausted at the end of my week, but I had made enough money to sort out my nose. I asked if it were possible for me to work over Christmas and matron said that although the rota had not been finalised, she thought it would not be a problem. Most nurses who have children want to be at home with the family. I agreed that I would call her or the agency that supplied auxiliary nurses to the hospice in late November/early December. It would be good if I could get the work because Christmas Eve and Christmas Day and Boxing Day all paid double time.

I slept on the train all the way back to Newcastle. It was hardly surprising because I'd gone straight from Lyndhurst Gardens to King's Cross when I came off duty and jumped on the first train. As soon as I got back to Leazes Terrace, I took to my bed. I needed to readjust my body clock. It was about three o'clock in the afternoon when I decided to get up and get myself something to drink. On my desk were three assignments, which were due immediately after half term. As I did not much like constitutional and administrative law, I decided to go back to bed, at least for a short while. By the time I woke up, it was early evening and dark outside. I switched on my desk light and, sitting in my knickers and bra, I settled down to complete the first of three assignments.

I had decided to go on a diet, because if I did not eat I could save my money and that was a very good reason for losing weight. During the following two weeks I cut down my intake of food significantly and by the time Louise came back I was a good three or four pounds lighter.

At the start of term I went to the common room early. Jo was sitting in one of the window seats; she seemed pleased to see me. She, like me, had done very little academic work during the holidays. She found Newcastle boring without her fellow students. Pauline Moulder joined us. One of Pauline's kids was not very well and she had been a little preoccupied with her child during the holiday. We all quickly fell back into our way of having a laugh, taking the micky out of the other students who thought that we did not behave as well as we ought. I did not tell anyone that I had worked in the hospice over the break. It would have provoked more needless questions. The second half of the term got off to a good start. I got an 'A' for an essay. Mr Stevenson said it was jolly good considering.

'Considering what?' I asked

'Considering the fact that you spent the holiday working.'

'Did I?' I asked, shocked and bemused that he knew.

'In the Lyndhurst Hospice.'

'How do you know that, sir?'

'Because the sister wrote to me, as your personal tutor, for a reference about you.'

'I did not know that,' I said.

'I'm quite sure that you did not, otherwise you would not have got away with it. University is about fun and in between all that fun, it's about hard work. You have to pace yourself Constance.'

'I will remember that, sir,' I said. 'But in any event it is a good essay mark considering.'

'Go on, shoo,' said Mr Stevenson. 'You are not the only student that I have to keep in line.'

Mr Stevenson was a good old stick. It was just as well he did not know the real reason for my working in the hospice.

Term took its course. I tried to resist the offers of parties and spent most of my time in my room or in the library. Twice I went to the pictures in the heavily subsidised film theatre. The two films I saw there were 'Waiting for God', which made me cry, and my favourite all time film 'Lace.' It was about a student who falls in love and is quietly driven mad, although her boyfriend, who has behaved very badly, is oblivious of her fragile mental state. I couldn't see myself falling in love if it did that to you.

As the end of term rapidly approached, I contacted the hospice to see if there was any work for me. There was. I was offered the opportunity to work from the day before Christmas Eve straight through to January 2. I asked if there was any accommodation. 'There might be,' was the reply, so I agreed to work. The whole Christmas scene was not a big deal for me, in fact I would rather not have to go through Christmas. I had never enjoyed it even as a child and now that I was grown up I would do anything to avoid it. I was quite convinced that no one would consider buying me a present and I doubted whether any of my family would even notice that I was missing. I had had no contact with my sisters or brothers since my move to Newcastle. I had no idea what my mother was up to. Whatever it was, it could not be any good. Sutherland Square was a million miles away. On the occasions when I thought about Sutherland Square, it was my bed that I thought about, my four-poster bed with my nice brown curtains. For a very brief period, that bed had made me happy, happier than I had ever been and now it was dismantled and stored in a cold warehouse awaiting my return.

I seemed to be getting on better and better with J. He made me laugh, but he did keep going on about his girlfriend. She seemed like a nice person. I don't think I was jealous, because I did not think of J as a potential boyfriend. I had not come to Newcastle to find a boyfriend. Besides, in the back of my head I still remembered the words my mother had said, when we had talked about my having children.

'Who would want to get into bed with you? What are you going to do when you do get into bed with your man? Piss on him? He will run a mile. Why would he want to get into bed with you when you will piss on him? As night follows day you will piss on him. Given time you might even drown him.'

'I will have children,' I had said, 'and when I do I'm not going to smack them. I will never hit my children.'

'You!' she said. 'Who the fuck wants to have children with you? I tell you what, bring them home to me. I'll save you the trouble of smacking them, I'll string them up from the nearest lamp post.'

Ever since, the thought of my children swinging from the nearest lamp post was enough for me to rule out relationships with members of the opposite sex.

There was a particular reason why I liked J. He was effectively on his own. He had lost his mum years ago. She had died suddenly and he did not get on with his father. So we had something in common, though he did not know it. I too had lost my mother years ago. She was not dead, but as far as I was concerned, my mother had not made a single useful contribution to my life. When I went into the common room, J always seemed to seek me out. It was a deliberate choice. Maybe the doctor was right. Maybe I was not so ugly after all. I was looking forward to the Christmas holidays. It was yet another opportunity to save up money for my operation. If J liked me now, he would like me all the more when I had my surgery. Easter could not come soon enough.

4
Merry Christmas

At the end of term the hall of residence was virtually empty. Most of the students had returned home, those remaining were foreign or, like me, had nowhere to go. It was at times like these that isolation and loneliness sent me out for a long walk around Newcastle to clear my head. It was bitterly cold. It had snowed on and off for the past week and Wellington boots were necessary. I walked to the centre of Newcastle and got myself a cup of tea. The shops were beautiful, full of pretty dresses and beaded cardigans. Pale pinks and baby blues were the 'in' colours. It had been a long time since I had bought myself any new clothes. The days when I was aware of the latest fashions had long passed. My Saturday job at Roses on the Walworth Road had equipped me with a fine appreciation of nice clothes irrespective of whether I could afford them! I still knew exactly what I would buy and wear were it not for the lack of money. I was hovering outside the shop by the reduced clearance box, when the shop assistant came out.

'Nice colours, aren't they? Autumn colours. See anything you fancy?'

'No,' I said unconvincingly.

'There must be something you fancy.'

'What? Sorry I didn't realise you were talking to me.'

'Nice and warm. Come in and take a look. We have some really good bargains on our reduced rail.'

'No thank you, I couldn't. I've got no money.'

'Just come and look – after all it's Christmas.'

I walked into the shop with my jeans tucked into my Wellington boots and a large knitted hat pulled down round my head. I looked like Newcastle's scruffiest bag lady. I was conscious that I was not dressed in the latest fashions and the shop assistants were.

'It's all lovely,' I said, 'but I could never afford it.'

'What about this rail?' she said, pointing to the 'everything must go' sign. As I fingered my way through the rail I found what I was not looking for: a loose pleated gypsy skirt in the colour of fallen leaves – pale burnt orange, a variety of shades of brown and tiny strands of golden thread interlaced in the fabric. I fell in love with it.

'That's nice,' I said.

'Try it on.'

'No, I couldn't.'

'It's reduced. It's the last one actually.'

'How much is it?' I said

'This one here is reduced to a tenner, but I'll do it for you for a fiver.'

That was certainly tempting.

'Have you got a top to match?' I said, boldly.

The assistant pointed towards some roll neck jumpers in orange, brown, blue, pink and red.

'What about this?' she said, picking up the orange jumper and holding it against the skirt.

'Both of them for a tenner,' she said. 'I must be overcome with the Christmas spirit.'

'What size is the jumper?'

She pulled out the label from the back. 'Size 12. They look lovely together.'

They did and I got my £10 out before she could change her mind. She wrapped my purchases and said 'Merry Christmas.'

'Merry Christmas,' I said, as I left the shop and made my way back to Leazes Terrace to try on my new clothes. They looked fine – both fitted me quite well. I decided that I would wear them on Christmas Day.

*   *   *

I travelled down to London on December 22 and went straight to 215 Camberwell New Road to find my father. I knocked, but the door remained unanswered. When he won the pools years ago, he had bought lots of houses in Camberwell and, though they were usually let out, he hung out in some of them. I went to Offley Road. He was not there. I made my way to his address at Ethnard Road. His girlfriend Delores had not seen him. I rang the hospice in Lyndhurst Gardens, but they did not have any accommodation for me. I made my way back to the Oval, just south of the river Thames. I had stayed there with Miss Lindsey on several occasions when I was much younger. I managed to find the block of flats, but had trouble remembering the exact door number. I rang three bells and knocked on three doors, but Miss Lindsey was not about. I had travelled light to London, with just a few books, my Christmas outfit, a change of clothes and my toiletries. It was now close to eleven o'clock and I was getting tired running around trying to find my dad.

I remembered that as a child I had on occasion passed through nearby Kennington Park and I knew that there was a way into the park. Part of the fencing had been dislodged and it was possible to slip underneath. I walked to the main entrance in St Augustus' Place. The gates were shut. I walked round the perimeter, but when I got to where I remembered the loose fencing, it had been repaired. I carried on walking and came across a new gap underneath the fence. I crawled under. I walked round inside keeping close to the perimeter until I arrived at the swings. Behind the swings I found dense bushes and a bench just as I remembered them. I placed my bag at the far end of the bench, lay down and gazed at the stars, using the bag as my pillow. I had never really looked at the stars before. Some people had argued that it was not possible to see the stars, because of all the pollution, but it was not true. Fortunately it was quite warm for the time of year and I was so exhausted I soon fell asleep.

I woke up at first light. The birds were chirping and I could hear the rats in the dense bushes behind me. The temperature had fallen during the night and I felt quite cold. My neck was stiff. Looking around me, I sensed that I was not alone. To my left there were another three, possibly four, men sitting on a bench, one with a large cider bottle in one hand and a can of Guinness in the other. The others were of a similar age, possibly late thirties or early forties. They all wore dirty trousers and shirts. It was not until the one with the bottle spoke that I realised she was female. Her front teeth were missing. Her hair was grey and her face orange and purple and mauve. I stayed perfectly still, not because I was intimidated, but more because I did not wish them to know that I was there. They appeared to be arguing over the bottle. A man in a duffle coat wanted the bottle back from the woman and had attempted to grab it on several occasions, only succeeding in swinging his arm into one of the others. Eventually he swung round so rapidly, he fell off the bench onto the floor and flat on his stomach. He had trouble getting up. Another man knocked the bottle out of the lady's mouth with a back handed swipe.

'I told you, you fucking bitch, not to drink it all,' said the man on the ground. Holding onto the arm of the bench, he got up in a half sitting, half standing stance and it looked as though he was uncertain whether to get up or sit down.

'See what you gone and done,' said the lady who was now bleeding from her mouth. 'I told yous all that I wouldn't fucking drink the lot and look.' She had an Irish accent. She wiped her mouth with the back of her coat sleeve, but the blood continued to flow. Part of the bottle had broken in her mouth. 'Ah Jesus!' she said. 'Where's me bottle?' The fourth person who was on the bench appeared to be asleep It was difficult to tell whether number four was male or female. Their skins were all weather beaten. The woman grabbed the bottle again.

'I'll leave some for yous,' she said wiping away the blood and taking a swig. As she did she kicked the fourth member. 'Are's

45

wake up yer piss artist.' His head swung back and he was obviously male. 'Wake up yer focker,' she said as she poured the drink over him. He didn't wake up. He snorted and groaned, but he didn't wake up.

'Why the fuck don't you lot shut the fuck up. We're trying to sleep,' said a voice to my right. There was no bench there, but in the bushes underneath the thick undergrowth I could make out a sleeping bag of sorts. There were two heads protruding from it.

'Shut the fock up yerself,' came the woman's reply. 'Who do you think yous are talking to? You don't know me, I don't know you and you telling me to shut the fock up, when you should be shutting the fock up.' She turned to her companions. 'Did you hear what he said? He said to shut the fock up.' She turned back to address the bushes. 'Now yous tell me what you gonna do about it. That's what I wanna know, what you gonna do about it?'

As she took another swig from her cider bottle she fell sideways onto the bench. The man who had been waiting for his go on the bottle snatched it and ran off. She struggled to her feet and ran after him, shouting and hurling abuse as he ran zig zagging away from her. As they disappeared into the distance, a calm fell over the park.

I remained on the bench, not quite asleep and not quite awake. Across the road from the park was a small cafe, which was open very early in the morning. I got myself a warming cup of tea and walked back to Offley Road. My father was still not there. I knew that in the centre of Camberwell there were some public baths, so I made my way there and had a bath. You are allowed one refill so I shouted out for my refill. When I had scrubbed myself clean, I went to the library to read until it was time to go to work.

The hospice was full to capacity and we had a Christmas tree up in the common room. Tinsel and paper stars hung in the corridor and around the doors and there were lots of Christmas cards strung in a card tree. The patients I had previously helped look after were no longer there. There were new ones in their place. The handover report identified several who were not very well at all and two of them were on oxygen. Their relatives had been informed that they should be on hand to return to the hospice if there were a sudden deterioration. Sister and staff nurse handed out the drugs. I got on with my duties of making the patients comfortable. Some of them were in a festive mood despite their poor condition. Others had piled high Christmas presents which they hoped to give out on Christmas Day. Two of the patients in the side rooms looked very unwell. Both were asleep with half open eyes and the skin over their cheekbones was paper thin. I did not disturb them because I would have caused more discomfort.

Two of the ladies in the four-bed rooms were looking forward to spending Christmas at home with their family. That was nice. Maybe one day I too would spend Christmas at home with my family. The men on the other side of the ward were in fairly good spirits. All had had a good day with lots of visitors. In the single ward the patient was asleep; I knew he was not well because he had been mentioned on the handover report. He was very thin and his bones stood out, but apart from that he looked fine to me. After the bedpan round and lights out everyone seemed to have a good night. There was not much to report.

Come eight the next morning, I was in desperate need of my bed. I took the bus to 215 Camberwell New Road and found my father in the garage at the back playing with his latest Capri. He was pleased to see me.

'La de da. How are you Clearie?'

'I'm fine,' I said, 'but I've got nowhere to live for the next couple of weeks.'

'What about University?'

'I'm on holiday.'

'What about Carmen?'

'What about her, George?'

'Well you can always go there.'

'That's not an option. Besides I only need somewhere for the next seven days and then I'll be going back up to Newcastle. You've got plenty of houses – surely you can find me a room somewhere?'

My father continued to play with his glove compartment. Lighting up a cigarette he said to me: 'You've not given me much notice, Clearie.' He went on opening and closing his glove compartment and then he started to switch the lights on and off. The Capri was in excellent condition, not a scratch, no blemishes and a silver blue colour under the gleaming polish.

'You should have given me more notice, Clearie,' he said.

'Never mind George,' I said. 'It doesn't really matter.'

I approached the car on the front passenger side, opened the door and pushed the seat forward. Before my father could stop me I was in the back of his Capri with my feet up on the back seat. Spreading myself out I said: 'Never mind, I'll just sleep here until you find something for me. Wake me up when you've found me a room.'

I pulled out the ashtray just to have a look, but the whole thing came away in my hand.

My father stared at me through the rear view mirror. He stared so long the ash from his cigarette fell off into his lap.

'Clearie,' he said. 'Clearie!'

I pretended to be in a restless sleep and brought the sole of my left foot up against the passenger side window.

'Clearie,' my father said raising his voice. 'Clearie, please do something for me. Please, I beg of you, just ease your foot away from the window.'

I ignored him.

'Clearie, Clearie dear, please take your time and come out of my car. You cannot sleep in my car. Please Clearie I have just the bed for you.'

'Where is it?' I said

'Come out of the car,' said my dad as he reached the passenger side door and pushed it open. 'Come out Clearie.'

'Where is my bed?'

'Just up the road,' he said. 'you've been there before. Miss Lindsey, you know Miss Lindsey. Come, Clearie, let us go, but please I beg of you, move your foot.'

I took my foot down and sat upright in the back of the car.

'Let's go,' I said.

My father's eyes focused on the print my foot had left on the inside of the window.

Miss Lindsey was not at home, but my father had the keys for her flat and when we went in I was astonished at how at ease he was there. He seemed to know where everything was.

'Will she not mind?' I said.

'No. She is away at the moment in Manchester, but I'll leave a note telling her that you are here.'

As my father wrote the note, I walked to the room which had once been mine. It was like stepping back into a dream. The room was exactly as I remembered it. The wallpaper was the same print, but now a little faded. There was a strong scorch mark on it in one corner and the net curtains could hardly be described as the finest. On the bed was a pink candlewick bedspread, similar to ones my mother had and under the bed was an enamel pottie. It was as if Miss Lindsey knew all those years ago that I would return.

'There is a spare set of keys on the table and if you eat anything please replace it. Miss Lindsey will not be back until the New Year. You might need some money while you are here.' He handed me two pounds. 'Please return the keys through the letterbox when you go.' My father started to sing as he made his way down the hall to the front door. 'Merry Christmas Clearie,' he said and with that he was gone.

49

Christmas Eve never did appeal to me much anyway. I had the most wonderful sleep on a bed that was warm and welcoming. A mattress that was thick, unlike my mattress at University. I fell into a deep sleep with my clothes on and the light on too. It must have been about five o'clock in the afternoon when I woke up. I had another bath and helped myself to some toast and tea. Before setting out for work I unpacked my Christmas clothes and hung them in the wardrobe in my room. My holiday assignments I left by the side of my bed. There was not much food in the fridge to last me six days; the milk was almost off and the cheese had mould all around it. Slipping into my uniform I made a note to get my Christmas shopping on the way to work. The Convenience Store was open, as was Boots the Chemist. I bought some potatoes, baked beans and cheese and a box of six deep filled mince pies, milk, teabags and bread. In Boots I bought a Christmas special of mascara and shimmer gloss lipstick to go with my Christmas outfit. I was now ready for the festive season.

Once at Lyndhurst Gardens, I left my shopping in the staff room behind the door, putting the milk in the fridge with a mental note to collect it on my way home. We had our hand-over report. No one had died and we had no newcomers. The two patients who had been unwell were now critical and both had their family members sitting with them. Day sister thought that we would lose them, but they were hanging on until Christmas. We settled the patients quite quickly. There was not a great deal that they required and once they had had their night caps and painkillers the lights were turned down and those of us who believed in Santa Claus waited for him to make an appearance. Shortly before midnight the light went on in one of the four bed rooms and I went to see what the matter was. The patient was sitting upright with her eyes half open. As I entered the room she barely raised her arm to indicate that she required attention. I switched her call light off and stood by the side of her bed.

'Hello,' I said, 'what can I get you?'

She said in a whisper, 'Nurse, will you please ring my son and tell him to come.'

'Of course,' I said. 'Do we have his number?'

She pointed towards her bag and I retrieved it from the chair. Fumbling in her bag, she handed me a piece of paper with a telephone number.

'Any message?'

'Tell him I require him.'

I confirmed the number with her and went off to get clearance from Sister. It was late and he may have been unduly alarmed by a call at that time of the night.

'No,' said Sister, 'if she requires us to call her son, then call him.'

I went to the staff room to make the call, but Sister said that she would do it. After Sister made the call, she told me he would be here within the hour. I went off to tell the patient, but when I got into her room she had fallen into a coma. She was certainly unconscious and by the time her son arrived the curtains had been drawn around her bed. She had died. He was grief stricken and sat with his head in his dead mother's lap crying, 'I'm sorry mama.' We did try to tell him not to blame himself, but he was having none of it. Other members of the family sent messages that they would arrive soon. That did not give us a lot of time. I was asked by Sister to sort out the body, to lay her flat, comb her hair, give her a final bed bath and a change of clothes before she was taken to the morgue. Once she was ready I then had to change all the bed clothes and wash down the bedside wardrobe, chest and table. The bed had to be re-made just in case we had another admission. It was six fifteen before that was all done and just as we were about to get a cup of tea Sister decided to do a ward check. Everything was fine until she got into the last but one room on the other side. Another of the lady patients had passed away in her sleep. I had not yet finished bagging up the belongings of the first deceased, when Sister told me to leave them and wash down the second body, because the relatives would be in any time soon.

This was really very stressful. It is not easy to give a newly deceased a bed bath or to change their clothes when you're working against the clock. I managed to do it and added bit of make up and blusher just in time before the first of the relatives arrived. She really did look very nice, as though she were at complete peace with all those who had irritated her in her former life. As the relatives gathered round the bed, I went to register the body at the morgue and to arrange for collection of the body and her worldly goods as soon as the last relative left. On top of all that I still had my other duties to perform. The other patients needed attention too.

By the time eight o'clock arrived I was still waiting for the body to be collected. I was so tired on the way home that I fell asleep on the bus and missed my stop. I had to walk part of the way back. When I hit the bed I did not wake up until after three o'clock in the afternoon. I got dressed in my Christmas outfit and prepared my Christmas dinner. I spent ages in the bath, having a long soak whilst my potato was baking in the oven. My gypsy skirt and jumper looked wonderful on me. So did the mascara, which made my eyes look bigger. The orange lipstick was another story – it was horrendous. I just did not have the right mouth for it. I made a note to get my mouth sorted when I could afford it. My mother was right. I did not get my mouth from her side of the family.

For Christmas dinner I had a nice jacket potato, baked in butter and foil, baked beans and mature cheddar cheese with a cup of tea. Well, it was two cups of tea, but no one was counting. Then I ate three mince pies. After that I watched telly until it was time to make my way back to Lyndhurst Gardens. There were very few buses running and even fewer trains so I set out early, intending if necessary to walk part of the way.

There was more bad news at the hospice. We had lost another two patients. They had drifted off shortly before seven o'clock and the day staff were so busy that they did not have time to sort out the bodies, although the relatives had been informed. The bodies had not even had a bed bath yet. After the handover report Sister told me not to bother with the tea or night caps, but to deal with the newly deceased and make them presentable to their relatives. That really was a bit rich, because I did not have a great deal of time and I was the only auxiliary on duty. Sister could not help, nor could staff nurse: they were far to busy giving out the DDAs (Dangerous Drug Administration), which really could not wait.

I was getting quite efficient at preparing bodies now and finished the job in forty-five minutes. They both looked happy and peaceful when their relatives came in. They stayed long enough for me to give the other patients a late night cap and settle them down for the night. Just after midnight the porters came and wheeled the newly deceased away. Sister gave me a hand to wash down the beds and get them ready for new admissions.

Christmas was soon over for me. After that at least it would be easier getting transport back to the Oval. The death rate slowed down after the festive season and by the time I was on the train making my way back to Newcastle we had only lost one other person, which was not bad. I had two weeks to get my work done before the start of term. I put my Christmas outfit in the bottom of my wardrobe. I no longer had any use for it. Best of all, I had earned a lot of money.

5
Under the Knife

1980

At the start of the second term our group seemed more relaxed, more at ease with the routine. We settled down to work fairly quickly. I hardly knew my room mate, Louise, and she hardly knew me, but despite that we seemed to get on well enough. I collected my grant as soon as I was able. I had already planned that I would spend it on my operation. I still had some money over from my previous term's grant. Now there were my savings from Lyndhurst Gardens and another large cheque for this term. After lectures ended on the first day, I re-read the letter informing me of the date of the operation: the first Wednesday after Easter. It had been some time since I had read the letter and I had not replied to it. Now I did.

January 1980

Dear Mr Anthony,

Thank you for your letter informing me of the date of surgery. I now write to confirm that I shall be available to be operated upon on that day and look forward to meeting you. In the meantime I enclose a cheque for the balance of the sum outstanding. Would you kindly acknowledge receipt by way of return.

Yours faithfully,

Constance Briscoe

I had no idea how I would manage my finances after the cheque had cleared, because it would almost wipe me out. At least my rent was paid, so there was no chance of being thrown out. I was on a diet anyway so this would just help me to lose more weight.

A new girl had joined our group, Alison Day. She was very pretty, very quiet and very ladylike. Unlike Jo and Pauline, she was not at all loud and, although she did occasionally drink wine, she was never drunk and I had never seen her even tipsy. I got on with Alison. She never spoke ill of anyone and was always willing to let you copy her notes if you had missed part of a lecture. We spent a lot of time chatting. She had two sisters who were younger than her, both of whom she got on with. I suppose I was drawn to her because Alison was very comfortable with herself in a way that I never had been. She spoke often about her home life and her parents and she was always keen to go home at the end of term. I found it extraordinary that there were parents around who their children actually liked and wanted to go home to see.

J told me he had broken up with his girlfriend over Christmas. I asked him why and he said it was just not working out and there came a time in life when people had to go their separate ways. At first I was sympathetic, but when I thought about it later I realised that J was actually telling me that he was available. Maybe he was interested in me. No body had ever been interested in me before. During our mid morning coffee breaks we found a way of sitting next to each other or he would buy me a cup of tea or I would buy him a cup of coffee. I felt very comfortable with him.

The doctor wrote back a few weeks later acknowledging my cheque and confirming my surgery. As the weeks raced towards half term we were all looking forward to the break. J was going back to Welwyn Garden City, but when I told him that I was staying up in Newcastle he said he would come back early. He did and we spent much of the time in my room. He made me laugh. Just before term started I invited him over to my house and cooked him a meal. It was rice and chicken, one of the few meals I could cook perfectly. It went down very well. He had no idea that I was such a brilliant cook. If only he knew. That night he stayed over in my room. Louise was still away. I was very happy about that. Early the next morning he went back to his own house.

At first no one knew that we were an item. We acted as if we were just good friends. Things continued exactly the same as before, but with one difference – at the coffee break J no longer asked me whether I wanted a tea, he would just get it for me and I would do the same for him. We never held hands or anything like that. Some of the girls in the year above who fancied J were quite taken aback when the rumour went around that we were seeing each other. I did not confirm or deny it and nor did J; it was our business.

At the end of each day J would come over to my house and eat with me. I did a very good chicken and rice. He, on the other hand, could produce any dish as long as it was covered in bolognese sauce. Sausage bolognese was not a dish that I had heard of, but J assured me that I had not lived. Once or twice I went to the Student Union to have a drink with him. He always drank beer from a pint glass. I started to drink from a half pint glass, lemonade and tonic water mixed. That way it was not so obvious what I was drinking and most people assumed I was drinking half a pint of vodka and tonic! I did not like the Student Union at all. It was crowded with people who had drunk far too much. Some of the male students were unable to walk straight and the girls were a bit dramatic with their arm movements. The air was thick with smoke that made my eyes water and the music was far too loud. I tried to avoid the Student Union although J thought it was fun.

By the time Easter approached we had a fairly settled relationship. Once or twice I had been over to his house. Like me, he shared his room with another student, and it was in a state! Clothes, books, leather jacket were thrown all over the floor. I had to step over his belongings to get to a chair. If I had allowed my room to get into that state, my mother would have beaten me silly.

I was sad when the end of term arrived and J went home to Welwyn Garden City. We promised we would keep in touch and meet up when I was in London. I could not give him an exact date, because I did not know how the surgery would work out. I did, however, promise to ring him at home every other night just to catch up.

After the other students had returned home, I was once again alone. Louise had gone home straight after her last lecture. I did not waste any time at all, but got down to prepare my Easter assignments. Over the next week I prepared skeleton essays in draft form for each subject and did some background reading from the list we had been provided with in the first term. I was pleased with myself. I had worked hard and was ahead with my preparation.

On the due date I finally arrived at the surgery in Harley Street. I had packed in accordance with my instructions – underwear, Vaseline, dark glasses and a change of nightdress. I did not have any specific idea what to expect, but I knew that at the end of the procedure I would look better than now.

I was greeted at reception by a nurse that I had not met before. She was very mumsy in a fashionable, upmarket kind of way. She embraced me warmly. I was shown into a waiting room with only one other patient. I tried my best not to stare at her, although I had a strong desire to give her the once over and try to guess what exactly she was having done. I could feel her staring at me, probably thinking the same. She would never guess in a month full of cosmetic surgery. A quarter of an hour later the nurse returned.

'Miss Briscoe,' she said. 'Would you like to follow me?'

I picked up my overnight case and followed the nurse out of the room down the stairs and into a two-bed bay.

She handed me a paper gown.

'If you get undressed and pop this on, the doctor will be with you shortly.'

She drew the curtains and disappeared.

Placing my bag on the bed I began to undress. I felt slightly nervous. No one in the world knew that I was there. I could die in my sleep and no one, absolutely no one would ever know that Constance Briscoe once existed. I stripped off and put my clothes in the wardrobe. Putting on my paper nightdress, I sat on my bed waiting for the doctor to arrive. I willed myself not to open the curtains. I was desperate not to talk to my cosmetic mate in the other bed and equally desperate to prevent her talking to me.

Mr Anthony pulled the curtains back and came in.

'Hello, Constance,' he said.

'Hello, doctor.'

'How are you?'

'I'm fine, doctor.'

'Did you have a good journey?'

'I had a very good journey, doctor.'

'Just a few matters we need to go through. You have been nil by mouth since midnight?'

'Yes, doctor.'

'And you have no allergies?'

'None, doctor.'

'Please look at this form and let me know whether anything has changed since you first filled it in.'

I looked through the form and told him there were no changes.

'Well, Constance, the nurse will come in a moment and take your blood pressure, weight, height and fill out another medical record. After that I shall return and take you through your consent form. Then you will be taken down to surgery, but before that happens the anaesthetist will want to see you. If you have any problems in the meanwhile, will you please let me know?'

'Yeah sure,' I said.

He swept out and the nurse soon returned and followed the

procedures he had outlined, including a blood test. When that had been checked, the anaesthetist came in. He was a large man with a red face.

'Hello there,' he said.

'Hello.'

'You all ready for surgery?'

'I think so.'

'Is there anything that I should know?'

'No,' I said. 'Is there anything that I should know?'

'Well, in a moment nurse will come for you and take you to theatre, where the surgeon and I shall be waiting for you. I will put a butterfly needle into the back of your hand. You will not feel a thing, just a little prick, and then we'll get you to count to ten. We'll keep you sedated so you will be aware of what is going on. The operation will take about one hour and once it is over you will stay in recovery, so that you can be observed, and then you will be taken back to your room. The surgeon will come and see you after the operation. There is nothing to worry about. We will see you in theatre.'

He was gone. Nurse reappeared about fifteen minutes later.

'You all ready?' she asked.

'Yes.'

'All your jewellery off?'

'Yes.'

'Hair tied back under surgical hat?'

She looked up, answered her own question and ticked her check list.

'You've drunk nothing?'

'No.'

'And your teeth – any false teeth?'

'They're all my own.'

'Right, if you pop up onto the bed, we'll go.'

I was wheeled to the theatre on a trolley. Mr Anthony was there in his surgeon's green overalls. He and the anaesthetist were waiting for me all scrubbed up. I slid off the trolley onto an operating bed and was covered with a green blanket to chest height.

'Put your hand down for me,' said the anaesthetist. I did so. 'Well done. Now turn it over, palm down.' I turned my hand over and almost immediately felt a very cold sensation and then a prick as the butterfly needle was inserted into my hand. 'Now count to ten for me.'

'One,' I said, 'two, three . . .' I tried to say four but the words simply would not come out. I could not stop my eyes from shutting. When I tried to move my arms they simply would not obey me. I felt a very drowsy sensation. I was not asleep, but yet I was not awake and I could hear perfectly all that was going on around me in the operating theatre. Somehow I managed to pull my heavy lids open. When I tried to speak I was unable to.

Mr Anthony had his back to me, scrubbing up and replacing his gloves. Standing next to him, the nurse was preparing a number of operating implements on a side trolley. The anaesthetist was preparing another injection. The nurse wheeled her small trolley over to my right. On it were a number of pairs of scissors and an open flat knife like a Stanley knife for cutting carpets. There were some bent needles and what looked to me like a few hammers of different sizes.

'We're all ready now, Constance,' said the surgeon. 'I'm just going to dislodge your nose.'

I did not know what he was talking about, but the anaesthetist came round to my left and injected a solution in the area of my nose. When Mr Anthony then felt my nose across the bridge, I could definitely feel his touch and when he shook the bottom of my nose, my flare as he called it, I felt that too.

'Ready, Constance!'

Picking up the middle-size hammer he started to bang the side of my nose. The first hammer blow was directly on to the side of my nose and it hurt, but I could not speak. I felt my insides go down to my toes and all of a sudden I no longer wanted cosmetic surgery. The second blow hurt just as much. I felt a whoosh sensation wash over me. It was like a very hot flush, exactly the same sensation as when I used to wet the bed. The third blow across my nose made it wobbly and the surgeon said, 'There we go' as he put the hammer down. 'This might hurt a little,' he said, as he put his finger and thumb into my nostrils and pulled my nose down. My entire nose followed his hand when he pulled on it and it was now elongated. He twisted the bridge of my nose with his other hand and I felt my nose moving around like a swing bridge, as he pulled it this way and that. My toes were on fire. I wanted to tell him to stop, but could not get the words out. The nurse stood over me with some cotton wool in tweezers and every now and then she dabbed the blood from my nose and put a cotton bud in a tray. She seemed preoccupied with counting them.

The doctor let go of my flares and, using both his hands, squeezed the cartilage at the bridge of my nose very, very hard. I winced, but he was oblivious of my pain as he narrowed and reshaped the bridge across the nose. He called for his scissors and they were handed promptly to him by the nurse. The doctor sliced through the underside of my nose on the left hand side and then on the right. The blood poured down my cheeks and dripped round to the back of my neck. The nurse picked up her suction tube and inserted it into my nose to vacuum up the blood as the doctor worked away. Once he'd finished with the outside of my nose, he inserted his implement deep into my nostril and carved away at the bridge.

I felt, at that moment, that Mr Anthony had lied. This was painful beyond belief and still I was unable to explain my pain to him. He had long ago stopped explaining to me what he was going to do next.

'Needle and thread,' he said as he put my nose back together again and started to stitch it in place. When he had finished the stitching he placed a narrow splint over my nose and secured it with bandages along the outer edge.

'All done,' he said, as I passed out.

*   *   *

It was late that afternoon when I came round. A nurse was sitting next to my bed, gently caressing my arm. I could not focus at the start; as I looked down the bridge of my nose, the splint, plaster and bandage obscured my vision.

'You've been a long time coming round,' said the nurse, as she checked my blood pressure and pulse. 'How are you feeling?'

I just nodded. My throat was sore. My eyes were swollen and painful and I was having trouble breathing.

'You feeling poorly?'

I nodded.

'Are you in pain?'

I nodded.

'Do you want some painkillers?'

I shook my head. The nurse fluffed up my pillows again, felt my pulse and went away. It was much later that I saw Mr Anthony. It was already dark outside. He came and sat on my bed. He told me the operation had been a complete success. It didn't feel like that to me. He said that though my nose was swollen, it would be in much better shape when the swelling subsided. He left me to get some sleep and said he would see me the following day. I was glad. My lips were very sore. Breathing was a major performance, not something that came naturally. The back of my head hurt, where the doctor had pressed down on my nose and forced me into the pillow. I could see a mirror directly ahead of me on the wall. I wanted to get up and look at my ugly face, but the fact of the matter was my ugliness would soon be a thing of the past.

When I woke up the following day, I was aware of Mr Anthony at my bedside. The pain in my head had subsided and my nose no longer throbbed.

'We've done a good job. You can stop being concerned about whether you're ugly,' he said.

'I'm not ugly now that we've started, doctor.'

He laughed at me.

'There is no pleasing some customers, but I told you I always had a funny feeling about you and I was right.' He checked my pulse, and examined my nose. 'The black eyes will go after a few weeks. Did you bring a pair of dark glasses?'

'Yes, I did.'

'Well you can wear them on the way home,' he said.

A nurse came in carrying a tray with a new set of bandages.

'We are just going to examine your nose, make sure it's setting nicely, and once we've checked you post operatively you are free to go,' said Mr Anthony.

'Good,' I said, 'because I've got work to do.'

'As for work, young lady, we suggest a complete rest.'

'Yes, I know you do.'

'And will you pay any attention?'

'Yes, of course, doctor, but I've got some assignments to do.'

'Promise me you will rest.'

'I promise.'

The nurse removed the bandages very carefully and the doctor examined my nose. It felt tender even though he did not touch it. Very lightly the nurse re-bandaged it and I was free to go.

When they had gone, I got out of bed and made my way to the mirror. I looked like an alien from Mars with my red eyes and swollen face. My back hurt, my legs hurt and getting on my feet made me feel shaky. I made my way back to bed, turned on my side and started to cry. In my head I still felt ugly. I could not help remembering when I had brought my school photographs home to my mother. They were ordinary school photographs of me in a grey jumper and white shirt with my school tie on, trying to put on a smile, because the photographer had told me to. I brought them home, a large six by four and a collection of smaller photographs, but my mother refused to buy them. She did not see why she should spend good money on photographs of me when I was so ugly.

'Who would want to look at the photographs of an ugly child, who?'

She was right. My stepfather, Eastman, had compared me to his black arse. They were both right. I took the pictures back the following day. It was difficult to believe that hammering and stretching my nose would have improved matters.

The next time I woke up, one of the auxiliary nurses was wheeling her trolley into my room.

'Do you want some breakfast?'

'No, I do not.' The very thought of food made me feel nauseous.

'Can I get you a drink?'

'No, thanks.'

As she wheeled her trolley out I got up and ran a bath, and packed my bags ready for my journey home.

As I walked out of the hospital entrance in my shades, I was aware of how stupid I must look. It was a dark overcast day. My large bandage also made me feel self-conscious. On the bus back to the train station, I sat at the very front to prevent other passengers staring at me. When I got off the bus no-one really paid that much attention. On the train I sat in a relatively empty carriage, covered my face and fell asleep. The only time I was disturbed was when the ticket inspector asked to see my ticket.

Back in Newcastle I relaxed just a little when I caught a taxi to Leazes Terrace. In my room I did not bother to get undressed. I got straight under the covers and there I remained until the next day. I was so relieved that Louise had chosen to go home. That was an option I had ruled out long ago. The following morning, apart from making myself a cup of tea, I remained in bed until the late afternoon, when I got up only to check if the swelling round my eyes had gone down. It had, but not by much. I had marshmallow eyes, white and pink and swollen. Over the next two weeks the swelling virtually disappeared, but the discomfort remained. I went for a post-operative check in Harley Street, when the splint and stitches were removed. Mr Anthony held up a mirror. I could see little difference, apart from the mark where the stitches had been. When I told Mr Anthony he just laughed. He said the whole point about cosmetic surgery was that it was cosmetic!

I took the opportunity whilst in London to travel to the nursing agency on Camberwell Green. I knew that they provided nurses to Lyndhurst Gardens and I was anxious to work as an auxiliary again. I had used all my student grant money on my operation. They informed me that they had work on the night shift at a number of hospitals and since I wanted weekend night work there would be plenty, as that was the least popular time for agency nurses. I filled out the application form and made an arrangement to call in every Friday, just in case they could place me somewhere on Friday and Saturday night. Of course, I made it clear that I was willing to work also during my holidays. I still had my uniform from Lyndhurst Gardens, but the agency gave me one of their own dresses to wear.

During the next two weeks I felt dreadful. I had headaches every day for a week and even after that they came back every now and then. Eventually the swelling settled down; apart from a faint line at the base of my nose no one would really have known how dreadful my ordeal had been.

I could not wait to see J. Unfortunately, we had not been able to get together during the holidays. I had tried to ring him every other day as agreed, but he was never in. I left messages, giving him a time when I would call back, but even then he was never in. I continued as agreed to call him until I had my surgery and even then I only missed a day. I had been keeping watch to check to see if the light was on in his room. The day before term started, the window to his room was open and later that evening the light was on. I thought that it was a bit strange that J had not come over, but then maybe it was just his room mate who had returned. I decided that it was not a good idea to go over. I did not want him to think that I was too keen.

On the first day of term I went over to the Law Department. Some third-year students and a few second years were milling around. Jo was in the library and when she saw me she came up from the basement to join me for a coffee. In fact I don't drink coffee; she had the coffee and I had tea. Whilst we were sitting in the window seat I saw J. He looked as good as ever in his leather jacket, his red jumper and his Doctor Martens. As he approached I caught his eye, but he ignored me. Maybe he had not seen me, so I waited for him to enter our common room. It seemed an eternity, but it must have been all of five minutes. When he came in, Jo said, 'Hi J,' but he did not reply. Instead of joining us, which is what he always used to do, he went and sat at the opposite end of the room, near the door.

'What's the matter with J?' Jo asked.

I did not know. He was certainly acting very strangely. We caught each other's eye; he looked away. I was embarrassed. I was not sure whether I had done something wrong, but this was not good. He had definitely seen me, there was no mistaking that, and still he did not come over.

As nine o'clock approached we all made our way to the lecture room and I sat in my usual seat, the first on the left in the front row down the central aisle. Alison Day sat in the first seat on the right down the centre aisle. J came in. I kept my head down, but not so far down that I could not watch him. He walked towards me, turned down the central aisle past me and never said a word. I was upset. I had been feeding him up with my chicken and rice and he had repaid me by supplying me with sausage bolognese and ignoring me. After the second lecture we had our mid morning break. I went out of the lecture hall first, to save J the trouble of walking past me. I got myself a cup of tea and left J's coffee on the side like we usually did. I made my way back to our seats with my back to the window and waited. He sure took his time. He did not enter the common room until there was only ten minutes to go and then he went straight to the counter, bought himself a cup of coffee, completely ignoring the one I had bought for him, and sat with his back to me as far away from me as possible. No one said a word but I knew what they were all thinking. I carried on as normal, trying hard to ignore J just long enough to give myself time to think, but Jo and Pauline were on to it straight away.

'Is everything, okay Constance?' Jo asked.

'Yes.'

'You sure?' said Pauline.

'Yes, I'm sure.'

When the final lecture of the morning ended, I collected my books and made my way back to my room. I needed time to clear my head. I went over the things that I might have done wrong, but I could not really identify one single thing. I truly did not want a confrontation, but it would have been nice to know what it was that caused J to ignore me. That afternoon J's behaviour did not improve and I was just too embarrassed to ask for an explanation.

Tuesday and Wednesday were a repeat of Monday and by Thursday the gossip in the Department among the students was that we had split up. Well that was news to me: J had not told me that was the case.

By Friday I was unable to concentrate and decided to go to the Department earlier than usual. I arrived at about eight o'clock and went to work in the library. It was my intention to work straight through to my first lecture at nine o'clock, but I decided to get myself a drink before the rush of students. I went upstairs into the common room and as I entered J was leaving, we bumped into each other at the door.

'Sorry,' he said in his coarse sandpaper voice.

'Excuse me,' I said as I made my way to the drinks counter.

I felt a complete fool. 'Excuse me!' What was that? Surely I could have thought of something better, like "What the fuck are you playing at J?" As for him, he could at least have said "Oh I see you've got a nice new nose," but he hadn't even noticed. That's men for you, I thought. But then nobody else noticed either. That was it really, we did not speak again for the rest of that term. I decided just to get on with my studies. If J did not wish to see me that was his loss. As Miss K would say, "Clare, you deserve better."

In the second week of term we were well into the business of ignoring each other, although most nights I would glance across to his room to see if I could find any clues to help me understand why he had dumped me without explanation. There were none really, but in the third week I could almost swear that I saw a woman there. My heart missed a beat. I reminded myself that she could be with J's room mate. In any event I was not at all sure that I had seen a girl. I thought I saw the top of her head, but I could have been wrong.

On the Wednesday, J was sitting in the window seat with Jo. There was someone else sitting on *his* right, but I did not recognise her. She was wearing a leather biker's jacket. Jo got up immediately and made her way towards me.

'Hi Jo,' I said.

I flicked my eyes around the room. The only person I did not recognise was the woman in the biker's jacket sitting in the window.

'Constance,' whispered Jo, her right hand half covering her mouth. 'Have you met J's girlfriend?'

'No, I don't believe I have. Who is she?'

'She's the one in the jacket next to him.'

'Oh,' I said, trying to sound cool, 'which Department is she in?'

'She's not a student – she's unemployed. She's come up

from London to stay with J. She's living with him in Leazes Terrace.'

So that was it. J's ex, now current girlfriend had obviously moved in to keep an eye on him. She must have known about me. She sat there like a praying mantis, ready to break my spine dare I glance at her man. J just pretended that this was yet another day in the Law Department. Men! I caught his eye. He looked awkward, but not embarrassed. If he could read my eyes, he would have known exactly what I was thinking. It would have been OK if J had said 'Sorry Constance, but no can do' or even just plain and simple 'It's over.' He didn't even have the basic decency to say, 'Constance, sod off.'

For the next few days the girlfriend turned up at the Law Department and sat in our seats. I think eventually someone complained about her presence and she stayed away. I have to say it was a bit of a relief. I tried to keep a low profile for the rest of term. I really did not want to fall out with J, or anyone else for that matter, so it suited me to ignore him completely. Funnily enough J had problems with that. I think he would have preferred a scene to make him feel better. At times I felt like stuffing my chicken and rice down his throat for the humiliation he had caused me, but in public I kept to myself and never spoke of J.

I was offered a job at Lyndhurst Gardens, but felt unable to take it. The stress of my situation had caused me to feel under the weather. It got a lot worse. I felt like my expensive nose begun squeaking involuntarily which really did get to me. I phoned the doctor and he invited me back down to London free of charge. When I took an early afternoon train on Wednesday to see him, he examined my nose and told me it was all in my imagination. There was nothing wrong with my nose. I travelled back to Newcastle. I did not think that it was my imagination, but I was pleased that my nose did not squeak.

Back in Newcastle I tried to concentrate on my studies and to ignore J. The only way I could cope was to pretend that J and his girlfriend did not exist. It was not long before I airbrushed them out of my life. I decided that was it – no more men at university. I was there to get a degree, not pick up a boyfriend. What could I expect, particularly when he came with hand luggage?

6
Teapot Lips

1980-81

I soon felt strong enough to return to the hospice at weekends. I really needed the money now. I did not regret the money I had spent on the operation, because despite J's rejection I did feel better about myself. As my first year at University drew to an end, I was so tired I would retreat to my bed as soon as I could. I had decided that I would not stay another year at Leazes Terrace, and requested a move to a women-only block of flats. Alison Day had applied to do the same and we rather hoped that we could share a flat together. As I packed up my belongings I had no idea where I would keep them in the intervening period. I did, however, know that I had a job starting at the Beefeater Gin Distillery in Kennington, near the Oval. One way or another I would be on that train back to London in order to start my holiday job. I had to revive my finances and save up for my next cosmetic surgery.

I had arranged to stay at Miss Lindsey's during the summer vacation. She was happy for the company and although she never asked for rent I paid her every week for my keep. At first she refused the money and said that it was a pleasure to have a law student living with her, but I had insisted that I would only stay if she accepted some money. Even though she continued to refuse, I left the money on the kitchen table and eventually it disappeared.

The Beefeater Gin Distillery was massive and on the first day we had to turn up early for an 8 am clock-in. There were about forty of us starting that day, all of us students. Ann Cody, who had been at Sacred Heart with me, was in the queue ahead of me with a friend of hers called Jackie Maloney, whom I had briefly met a long time ago. My job was making up cardboard boxes. They came down from an overhead conveyor belt in flat packs and, together with eight other women, I would assemble the boxes and put innards in them and replace them on a conveyor belt. The boxes would then make their way along the conveyor belt, where another six women were waiting to fill the boxes with bottles of gin that came down at speed on a conveyor belt in front of the boxes. The bottles had on them a picture of one of the Beefeaters who guard the Crown jewels in the Tower of London, in his original sixteenth-century costume. Once the boxes were full they would continue along the conveyor belt, passing through a small hole in the wall to the packing area where the men would check the boxes, seal them and place them on large wooden crates, where they were piled six high. The fork lift driver would secure the crate and take it away to the warehouse where it would be stored awaiting distribution.

Ann Cody and Jackie Maloney were not on my conveyor belt. Ann had been given a job checking the bottles after they'd been filled with gin. This meant that she would put the bottle on a swinger, which would turn it upside down behind a large magnified plastic screen. Any debris or foreign particles that should not be in the bottle could be easily detected and removed at this stage. Jackie's job was to make sure that the bottle tops found their way to the top conveyor belt, facing the right way up, so that they would fall down onto the bottles. Further down the conveyor belt a separate machine would screw, or compress the tops into place. It was very hard work. We were allowed a twenty-minute tea break in the morning and afternoon and an hour for lunch and that was it. The full-timers were quicker than us, but the students got on with the job as fast as they could because the pay was good. The work did make your arms ache.

At lunch time I caught up with Ann Cody who was now at Queen Mary's College, London doing a degree in chemistry.

She was predicted a first. Jackie was studying sociology at some other university. I felt a sense of solidarity with them, particularly Ann, who had a difficult mother. Ann told me she still lived at home because she could not afford to leave, which made me feel quite lucky.

At the start of the new university year in September, I felt confident in myself. My new flat in the women-only block was lovely. Alison was one of my flatmates. The others I did not know, but they seemed to know one another. My room was no bigger than the one I had as a first year student, but I had it to myself, which was worth a thousand large rooms.

My group all felt very superior as second years. The first-year students in the law department looked fresh-faced innocents straight from school. They were rather better behaved than we had been. One day early in the autumn term, whilst I was in the common room drinking a cup of tea and eyeing up the new intake, I caught sight of J out of the corner of my eye. He was wearing the same old leather jacket and Doc Martens. He was as handsome as ever and I could not bring myself to dislike him, even though he had humiliated me when there was no need for it. He caught me staring at him. I think we were both quite embarrassed. He certainly flushed and I averted my eyes, but just for a moment. When I looked back he was still staring. Maybe he still fancied me. To be honest, I still fancied him, but I would never ever let him know that. I certainly did not want to pick up where we ended it, or I suppose it was more accurate to say where *he* ended it. I quickly scanned the room for his woman. She was not there. Something told me they had parted, but that was not my problem. My J days were over.

Jo, Pauline, Alison and I decided to go off for a pint. There was much to talk about. It had been a long summer. Some of the group we fell in with commented that I looked well. It couldn't be the colour of my skin, so it had to be a result of my cosmetic surgery. Although not one single person had actually noticed that I had had surgery, I was convinced that it had made me more attractive. We soon settled down to hard work. The results in our second year would count towards our final grade. From now on everything was for real. I was on my way to being a proper lawyer.

It was the middle of the first term before the nursing agency offered me a job at St George's Hospital or one at an old people's home at the back of Love Walk in Camberwell. I chose Love Walk. I had to cover Friday and Saturday nights, which suited me perfectly. I contacted my father, who said that I could stay at Miss Lindsey's on Saturday night. It was better than staying in Newcastle, where there was little to do apart from getting drunk and going to parties. It was when I was brushing my teeth on the first Saturday night of my new job that it occurred to me that I needed to sort out my mouth. The doctor was right. It looked like a teapot spout. As soon as I got back to Newcastle I wrote to the clinic in Harley Street.

Dear Mr Anthony,

You may recall our meeting when you operated on my nose. We also talked about my mouth and the scars on my face. The operation on my nose was a great success and I had no post surgery problems. I am now looking forward to having my mouth altered as we had agreed. I enclose £50 deposit and look forward to an early appointment. I have a half term coming up when I am available for surgery; after that, Christmas would be a good time.

Will you please let me know by way of return.

Constance Briscoe

PS Would you please bear in mind that I am a student when you estimate the costs.

I hoped that the doctor would not write back too soon, because I was not at all sure that I had the money to finance the operation. I had left myself very short the last time and then had to spend many of my weekends working, which I did not want to do again. It had been a while since I thought about Miss K, but the minute I thought about cosmetic surgery she was back again wagging her finger.

'No, Clare, no. This is completely unnecessary and a waste of money.'

'But Miss K,' I heard myself reply, 'surely it is no better than I deserve?'

'No, Clare, no.'

Miss K would not compromise, but neither would I. I could still hear my mother's words ringing in my ears: 'She is ugly, ugly, ugly. Where did she get that mouth from? She did not get it from my side of the family.'

The reply came back from the doctor in ten days.

> Dear Miss Briscoe,
>
> It was very good to hear from you after all this time. I hope that you continue to excel at your studies. Thank you for your deposit and please accept this letter by way of acknowledgement. We operate on a Wednesday. Although it has been some time since I last saw you I have looked at your file and reminded myself what we discussed at that last consultation. I am prepared to see you at the Harley Street Consulting Rooms free of charge to update any relevant developments prior to surgery. If it is more convenient to you, I have enclosed a comprehensive list of questions I would like you to deal with and return immediately.
>
> I look forward to hearing from you in due course.

The letter was typed, and I imagined the doctor typing away with his silk fingers. I did not want to imagine him operating on my mouth. That ordeal was not worth thinking about, but the more I tried to put it out of my mind, the more it came back to the forefront. What if it went all wrong? What if I looked hideous? What if the knife slipped and the doctor left me with a lopsided slanty lip? I decided that the risk was too great, so I penned another letter to the doctor.

Dear Mr Anthony,

Thank you very much for your letter and kind invitation to see you at Harley Street. Whilst it is probably not necessary, I would be grateful if you would arrange to have a consultation with me on the morning of the surgery. I enclose the form duly completed. There are a few issues that I am worried about, but I am sure they can be resolved on the day. I would like to book the first Wednesday of my half term, which is three weeks away.

Constance Briscoe

The reply came from a nurse, who made it clear that she expected to see me on the agreed date shortly after eight in the morning for a consultation with the doctor. She gave me a list of items to bring, including a loose fitting blouse, some icepacks and a spare pair of knickers in case I had a little accident. The operation did not require an overnight stay and, provided all went well, I would be available to be collected sometime after six o'clock. It was not desirable to drive myself and if I so wished they were more than willing to provide transport for me. Finally I should refrain from eating or drinking from midnight prior to surgery. I booked my train fare immediately to get a reduced price.

As the term progressed, I tried to concentrate on my work and to blot out all thoughts of surgery. One day however, I was convinced that Miss K was in my room. I woke early and it was half light. I was awake but not yet clear in my head. My face was turned towards the wall. I felt a light tapping on my foot, like a school teacher with a ruler tapping on the edge of the desk to draw the student's attention to some relevant point. The tap was not continuous, nor was it rhythmic. It only came when I was nodding off to sleep again. I assumed that it was my imagination. I lay with my eyes open, not daring to look. My eyes closed again and as I was getting comfortable, I felt another tap on my leg. Still I did not turn. The atmosphere in my room was warm, cosy and friendly. My bed was warm and I began to nod off again. Then I felt a cool breeze, as though someone had blown ever so gently on my face, slightly ruffling my eyelashes. I opened my eyes in an instant. I felt an air of expectation. Something had just happened, but I did not know what. I kept my eyes open, not blinking, not moving. I daren't look behind me. I started to get frightened and my stomach dropped and my heart felt as if it were falling into a void. Then I felt the cool breeze again. Whatever it was had come quite close to my face and was behind my right ear. Then the tapping started again. Once, then two double taps, and then several in rapid succession. I panicked and felt in danger of wetting the bed for the first time in years. I covered my face with my duvet and hoped and prayed to the good and gracious God that I had known for ever such a long time to give me courage.

I was aware of the duvet being pulled down the bed. A gentle tug at first. The second tug exposed the top of my head and then, as it slipped gradually through my hands, I suddenly felt exposed and cold. I turned to the right, away from the wall. I started to focus on the bottom of the bed. It was difficult to make out shapes and colours, but I could make out the outline of a person. It was definitely her. As she came into sharper focus, I could see her pitted skin. Miss K was sitting on the bed, half on and half off, with part of her right leg resting on the bed. The lilac and green twinset with its fine knit I would recognise anywhere. I opened my eyes more, but Miss K was not looking at me, she was tapping on my leg. I could not see her left leg; it was obscured because of the angle at which she was sitting. Then it occurred to me that it was not a question of not being able to see her other leg – she just did not have one. The space for her other leg was empty.

It was daylight. I was in bed. Yes, this was my room. Now I knew it was Miss K, I was no longer afraid. It was just like the good old days before her accident, when we talked about nothing in particular.

'Miss K,' I said. 'Miss K, it's me, Clare.'

Miss K did not say a word and she never acknowledged me. She just raised her hand and again tapped on my leg.

The colour of her hair seemed unreal. The faint smudge of lipstick was typical of Miss K, completely understated. She looked as I had always remembered her. She was Miss K. It suddenly occurred to me that the reason Miss K had ignored me was because I had not shown her respect.

'Miss Korcinskje,' I said. 'I'm sorry. It's me, Clare. Don't you remember, Miss?'

She turned to face me. We locked eyes and for the first time I saw she was crying. The tears had filled some of the contours of her pitted skin. They ran down her twinset and then onto the back of her hand. I started to cry too. She had come all the way to Newcastle, was sitting on my bed and yet she could not say 'Hello Clare.' When I lived with her she had told me that there was a big world waiting out there for me. She said I should go and never look back.

'Oh Miss K,' I said, 'what have I done? Why don't you talk to me?' I wiped away my tears and when I opened my eyes again Miss K had gone, disappeared.

I shouted to her to come back. Was it a dream? My leg did feel as if it had been poked and prodded. Looking down towards the bottom of the bed, I saw there was definitely a circular compressed area where Miss K had sat. It was not my imagination. Miss K had been there. I was distraught that she had not spoken to me. There was complete silence in my room. It was time to get up and get ready for class.

The rest of the day was so dull, the lessons so unexciting. I had Miss K on my mind and she would not go away. It was possible that Miss K was not happy with the surgery that I had lined up, but she had not said so. I was still determined to go through with it. For the rest of the week I went home straight from classes. I never went for a drink with Jo or the others. I was half hoping that Miss K would be there waiting for me but she never was. At the end of half term I packed my bags with just those items I would need for the clinic, checked my room one final time and made my way to the train station.

When I arrived at the clinic, I was led into the very same room I had entered when I had my first operation. There were three ladies already waiting. Putting my bag down, I got myself a cup of tea from the machine and, looking beneath my eyelids, eyed them up. All three of them were very beautiful, lovely proportions with no obvious defects that I could see. All three were reading magazines about beautiful women just like themselves. I remembered that I was not supposed to drink, so I put the cup down. I occupied myself by looking at the paintings on the wall. They were very unexciting pictures of trees set against a background of pink and mauve. In fact I decided that they were truly dreadful and it was a surprise that the doctor, whose delicate hands produced such beauty, should have chosen such awful paintings.

Nurse popped her head around the corner and asked one of the other ladies to follow her. I waited until Nurse returned with a similar invitation to me. I was led to the consulting room and as I entered the doctor was up, out of his chair, and making his way towards me.

'Please come and sit down. Well, it must be a while since I last saw you. Now let me see. It healed very well. Look at that nose, it's perfect.'

I would not have gone as far as to say perfect but it was certainly an improvement.

'I bet you don't remember what your nose used to look like.'

'I think I do, doctor, but I would rather not remember.'

Reaching round behind him, he picked up one of three photos that were in a row on his desk.

'That', he said, 'is your before photograph.'

He held it up in front of me and he was right. I did not recognise my nose.

'That never was my nose,' I said.

'Well, Miss Briscoe, you would be very surprised, but they all say that.'

I looked again. My nose was never that awful.

'This,' said the doctor, 'is your nose just after surgery. I believe it was a week or two later and you can see the date.'

In the photograph, my eyes were bloodshot and unfocused. My nose was swollen and quite bulbous. Compared to now, that 'after' photograph looked more like a 'before.'

'It is definitely an improvement doctor', I said. 'But what can you do about my mouth? Where did I get a mouth like that from?'

'Don't be so harsh on yourself,' he said. 'It really is not that bad.'

'Oh, but it is doctor.'

'You are determined to go through with this?'

'Yes.'

'You don't want to wait until you are older?'

'No. Absolutely not.'

'And the operation will make you feel better about yourself?'

'Oh definitely, doctor.'

'Well in those circumstances what I intend to do is this. First we will operate on the lower lip.' The doctor produced a rough sketch of an enormous pair of lips from behind him. 'You see here and here,' he said, pointing at the corners of my mouth.

'Yes.'

'We will inject here and here to relax the muscle in the lip, because the lip is literally all muscle, and once the lip is relaxed we will cut out as much tissue as we possibly can from this point here, to this point here. There is one problem.'

'What is that doctor?'

'We have to be careful that we do not cut into any muscle because that is not the purpose of the operation. We also have to be careful to leave the lips even and smooth, not lumpy. We just have to make sure that the tissue is removed evenly, otherwise you will be left with very irregular lips. If you don't mind I would just like to mark out the distance now. Nurse.'

He held his hand out and she handed him a strange looking ruler with a pair of claws with marks in inches and centimetres running along the edge of each claw.

'Push your lip out for me. No, no, not both, just the bottom one.'

I pushed my top lip in and my bottom lip out.

'Thank you,' he said, 'and if you would just hold it there.'

Nurse was busying herself around the room.

'Nurse,' said the doctor, 'please mark and note.'

The doctor read out some measurements and she made a note and read them back. The claws were clipped onto my lip starting at the left hand corner and every half a centimetre the doctor shouted out a measurement. When he had finished he thanked me and then went round to his side of the desk.

'I don't think we need any more "before" photographs,' he said, 'but what I might do is just mark out the area that we have to play with and that way we will know when we get close to the muscle.'

He did that and checked there was no change from the declarations on my record for the first operation.

'Well in that case why don't we ask nurse to show you back to your room and I will see you shortly.'

I thanked the doctor and nurse walked ahead of me as I was taken to a two-bed ward. The other person in the room was a large lady, in fact the first thing you noticed was how large she was. She sat upright in bed, the corners of the counterpane pulled up to just under her bust and held in place by her folded arms. The nightdress was hospital green and hung loosely around her neck. Her face was quite tubby, with no cheekbones and her hair was a grey afro. Her eyes were badly swollen and above both her eyelids was a streak of raised clotted blood red and mauve in colour. There was a linear track criss-crossed with tiny stitching held in place by equally tiny white plasters. Even if she had wanted to open her eyes I doubt very much whether she would have been able to.

'Here we go,' said the nurse as she pulled the curtains round my bed. 'You know the drill. I'll be back later.'

'Thank you, Nurse.'

I placed my bag on my side table and started to strip. I had brought my own nightdress, but I did not want to get it bloody. In any event, there was a freshly ironed hospital green night-dress on the bed. I put all my personal belongings in my bag and placed it in my locker. I kept my make-up mirror. I had my own way of remembering my before and after images. I placed the mirror in the drawer of my cupboard and hopped back onto the bed. No sooner was I there than the curtains were drawn back with a flourish and the doctor and the anaesthetist entered. I had not met him before. The latter went through his usual checklist and gave me a pre-injection in the back of my hand.

'We'll scrub up now and see you in about twenty minutes.'

I had been through all this before and I really did not mind at all.

Shortly after that we made our way to surgery. There really was no need for me to be wheeled in so the nurse agreed I could walk. As before, they were all there waiting for me. The doctor, the anaesthetist and the nurse had all scrubbed up and were wearing gloves and face masks.

I made my way over to the operating table. Nurse gave me a steadying hand to get up. I was trying to make sure that I looked decent. My hospital gown was open the entire length of the garment and tended to flap open when I walked, exposing my bottom.

'Are you comfortable?'

'Yes I am.'

'Are you feeling OK?'

'Yes I am.'

I got my main injection and was told to count to ten. I got to three before I felt a cold rush of tiredness go up my arm and, although I was still counting in my head I was not sure that I was actually saying anything. I could still hear and see everything they did. The nurse handed the doctor the largest syringe I had ever seen. The needle attached to it must have been at least four inches long. The doctor turned the syringe upside down so that the needle was pointing up and applied pressure on it with the plunger. Solution burst out of the eye of the needle. He repeated the action before approaching me and when he did I immediately felt sick.

'Now Constance,' he said. 'I am just going to loosen up your mouth so I will inject a solution that will make your lips feel numb. It will just be a tiny prick. OK, here it comes.'

I wanted to say 'Can you just hold on a moment doctor?' But I could not speak. I was in a twilight zone all of my own. The doctor inserted the needle into the left hand corner of my bottom lip and once the tip was in he forced the needle along the length of my entire lip and it did hurt. Once he reached the other side, he pressed the plunger and instantly my lip felt cold. As he withdrew the needle my lip expanded like floppy jelly on a hot summer's day, leaving my lip almost twice its original size. The doctor did exactly the same thing from the right hand corner of my mouth and then repeated the whole process again with my bottom lip. By this stage, I was in quite a lot of pain, although every time the doctor inserted the needle he told me that it was not going to hurt. I wanted to say, 'It's all lies doctor, it does hurt,' but the words failed me.

Once my lips were all floppy, Nurse handed the doctor the

claw-shaped measuring device that I had seen earlier that day, and as the doctor mapped out his path I could only wait in pain to see what he would do next. My mouth had flopped to the side, like a squashed-up pancake. Once the doctor was satisfied with his markings he returned the claw measure to the nurse, who promptly handed him a pair of scissors.

'No,' said the doctor, 'knife first.'

The nurse switched the scissors for a knife-like instrument and the doctor proceeded to cut open my lip, using the left hand corner as his base. The pain after the first incision was quite indescribable and I felt a rush of warm blood spout out of my lip like a fountain. It did not get very far because nurse was at the ready with her hose to hoover up the blood at the base of my lip. The doctor cut his way with painstaking precision all the way round to the other side and as he did so he kept talking to me. I did answer, but I am not sure that he actually heard me.

'That's done,' said the doctor. 'Now I'll just remove the tissue, Constance, and we'll be finished in no time.'

The knife was replaced with a pair of scissors and the doctor snipped away at my lip. At one point, he cut a large piece of tissue away and when he tried to remove it he was unable to, because it was still partly connected to my lip. The doctor used a pair of surgery tweezers to remove the tissue and as he held it up I saw a long strip of flesh, bloodied and raw. That was my lip, I thought. I hoped that my lip would survive the intrusive assault and would end up perfectly shaped. We must have had about forty minutes of snip time when the doctor finally put down his scissors and asked for a needle. Nurse had it ready and waiting for him, already threaded. Twenty-five stitches were put in my top lip and a significant number of additional stitches were inserted internally.

I was propped up sufficiently to see my bottom lip: it looked massive. I had never imagined that a lip could be that big. Now that is what I would call ugly!! The doctor finished the last of the stitching and started on the bottom lip. As Nurse handed him the knife, my heart took a turn for the worse and I passed out. I have no recollection about this part of the surgery apart from the doctor telling me that it would not hurt. Hours later, when I woke up in recovery. I could see perfectly well, but I was unable to talk. My lips were on fire and they were hugely swollen. I don't know what time it was, but when I came round again nurse was there at the side of my bed. She wanted to know if I was all right. I nodded. She said that I would feel a little uncomfortable, but this was normal. I nodded weakly. She told me that the doctor would be around later and right now I should try and get some more sleep. I was not able to answer the nurse. Had I been able, I would have told her that it was impossible to sleep when I was in that amount of pain. I managed to get the drawer of my cupboard open and felt around for my mirror. I had a good idea what I should expect, but it was much worse that I could ever imagine. My stitches were swollen to bursting and my mouth was more trout like in appearance. I had blood smears running down my chin from the corner of my mouth to the back of my neck and crustations of blood in the corners of my mouth. Looking at myself, I had a vivid flashback to the house in Sutherland Square. I was in the kitchen. I had brought home my school photographs, a collection of them in various sizes with instructions that if my parents wanted to purchase them, the money should be placed in a brown envelope which came with the photographs. If they were not to be purchased then they should be returned. I had shown them to my mother. I thought they were OK but my mother did not think so. Taking the photograph and holding it to the side of my face, she called my sister Pauline.

'Come quick.'

'What mummy?'

'Look P, tell me what you see.'

'That's Clare, mummy.'

'No, silly, tell me what you see.'

'It's Clare, mummy.'

85

'No, silly,' my mother said. 'Eastman come, look, tell me what you see.' Eastman came into the kitchen

'Make me see,' he said, looking at the photograph and back to me. 'Jesus fucking Christ, you is ugly ugly ugly.'

'Now,' said my mother, 'why do you want me to buy these photographs when you is so ugly?'

'I don't want you to buy them.'

'Well, if you don't want me to buy them you had better take them back.'

I returned them to Miss the next day.

'Mummy doesn't want them,' I said. 'The colouring is too dark and it does not bring out my best features.'

You is ugly, ugly, ugly that is true, I said now, looking at myself in the mirror. That is certainly true. I put the mirror back in the drawer and began to cry. The doctor came in and was a little startled.

'Constance, are you in pain?'

'Yes,' I said, not quite telling the truth, 'just a little doctor.'

The doctor told the nurse to get me some painkillers. Sitting on the edge of the bed, he looked at his masterpiece.

'You know, Constance, I am very pleased with the outcome. We've got good symmetry and it will heal with good defini-tion.' Checking the corners of my mouth the doctor added: 'The swelling will go down over the next couple of days, but it will take months to completely disappear. For the next ten days I advise no hot drinks and only drink through a straw – that will make things more comfortable for you. Apart from that, Constance, do you have any concerns?' I shook my head. 'Well what I suggest is you stay here and rest. Nurse will give you some painkillers, but stay until early evening. Then we can review the position and you can arrange for someone to pick you up.'

The lady in the next bed had gone. All her things had disappeared. I was once again all alone. I dozed off and when I awoke I saw Nurse must have brought the drugs in because I found them on my bedside table. I took them with some water and then dozed on and off. Gradually the pain eased. When six o'clock approached, I started to get ready to leave. I did not have anyone collecting me and I was a little embarrassed by this. I thought if I got ready and waited in reception for an imaginary friend, who was going to pick me up, I could just disappear while the nurses were occupied.

I slipped downstairs and sat as if I was waiting for someone. When the receptionist turned her back, I did a runner. As I made my way down Harley Street, the blood was seeping out of my stitches. Three slabs of blood had formed crustations round them. I kept my head down as I walked. On the Underground I could feel everyone looking at me. I pulled my jumper up to just under my chin and my sunglasses down to the bottom of my nose. At least that way no one would recognise me should we ever meet again. I finally made it to the train and found an inside seat at a table for four. I turned my head to the window and kept it there for the entire journey, even when the ticket collector came round collecting tickets. Cold and hot drinks were completely out of the question my lips were red hot, swollen and bulbous. I felt the stitches could burst at any moment. I was fairly certain that I would look better after a good night's sleep. In the taxi back to my hostel, I could see the driver staring in his rear view mirror at the monster in the back, a living horror story that he had just picked up.

I took more painkillers and quickly fell asleep. I stayed in bed for the whole of that day and the next, and when I was thirsty I sipped cold tea through a straw. Food was not on the agenda for now and to be honest, I did not feel hungry. It was probably about day three that the swelling started to go down. I had a lot of loose skin on my lips and by day four it was obvious that they would have a nice shape once the swelling had gone. Once I was feeling better I looked at my task for the holidays. There was quite a lot of reading to be done which could be accomplished in bed. During the next few days all the swelling disappeared and I was completely happy with my new appearance. When I looked in the mirror, my nose looked fine and I could see my mouth would look great. Now I was conscious of the scars on my face. I would have to do something about them next.

7
It's a Dirty Job . . .

On the Thursday there was a message for me to call the nursing agency. They wanted someone to work at Lyndhurst Gardens on Friday and Saturday nights. Sunday was optional and I accepted. This was a useful reminder of my financial circumstances. I was looking half way normal and the stitches were beginning to dissolve. No one stared at me on the train journey, which pleased me.

My troubles were nothing in comparison with the patients at Lyndhurst Gardens. We did not have a full ward. Quite a few of the patients had gone home for the holidays and would be returning on Monday. Two patients had died the day before and one patient was close to death. As we gathered in the staff room it occurred to me that after all these years I had never seen a patient make a complete recovery. That was really sad.

There was nothing out of the ordinary with the handover report. I did my round of tea and then bed pans, while Sister and the nurse administered drugs. I was surprised to see just how active some of the patients were. In one four-bed ward the lady first in on the left was in the process of putting her curlers in for the night. When I asked her if it was comfortable sleeping with curlers, she said that she would suffer any indignity to look her best. I knew what she meant

'Do you want a bed pan?' I asked.

'Well, that is an indignity that I will not suffer,' she said. 'I'll walk if you give me a hand.'

'Sure.'

She took hold of my arm and the pair of us shuffled to the toilet and back. The lady opposite was removing her make up and had the moisturizer piled high on the side table. She had beautiful china smooth skin.

'Can I get you something?' I said.

'Just a man, luvvie' she said, 'although heaven knows what I would do with him.'

The other two ladies started to laugh.

'I know what,' said the lady in the third bed, 'why don't you make that two and then we can go halves.'

All the ladies joined in the laughter. Some made saucy suggestions about which half they preferred, which led to even more hilarity. They all wanted a cup of tea and a refill. One of them shouted out that I should leave the teapot there with them. It was good to see ladies, even though they were seventy and very ill, in such good spirits. They all knew why they were there, what illness had brought them to the hospice and I was sure they knew that eventually the illness would overwhelm them.

The lady on the side ward, however, was not so cheerful. Her curtains were closed, the blinds drawn and the light off. Her hair was a beautiful fading blond with strands that appeared almost golden. The pillow behind her head looked badly creased and damp, which was probably due to the oxygen mask that covered her face. The oxygen hissed out of the transparent mask and I could see a film of tiny air bubbles rise from the top of the mask and disappear. Her eyes were half open, but it was clear that she was asleep. Her skin was yellow and drawn as tight as it was possible to be; not one single crease of skin could I detect on her face. There seemed to be a massive hollow where her neck should be. I very gently put my hand over hers and stroked the back of her hand. As she turned in my direction she smiled and a vapour of bubbles shot up in the air.

'Can I get you anything?' I said. She shook her head. 'How about me sorting out your pillow?' Again she shook her head.

'I'll change your water jug and take your cups if that's all right with you.'

As I walked over to her side table to collect the cups, I was conscious of her eyes following me around the room.

'What's your name?' she said almost in a whisper.

'Constance,' I said, 'but a lot of people call me Clare.'

'Constance,' she said, 'that's a very English name.'

'Yes, it is.'

'Constance, please don't worry about sorting me out.'

It was difficult to hear what she said, so I bent my right ear towards her. She removed her mask by pulling it down toward her chin.

'Please don't worry,' she said, 'I shan't be here for much longer.'

'Are you planning on going away?' I said.

Looking at her, huddled up in the bed with her knees raised as if on a pillow, I noticed that she had the Bible open on her lap. I could not see what passage she was reading, but as a bookmarker she had a rosary.

'Constance,' she said, 'you and I both know that I don't have long to go. My work here is done and soon I shall be with my Maker. So, Constance, I have no need for water or to be made comfortable. Please pray for me.'

I didn't know what to do. We had never been told how to talk about death with the patients. Quite a lot of them were so overwhelmed by their illness that they died readily accepting their destiny. I felt very sad for her and started to cry. The tears ran down my face and made my lips sting and, as I tried to press my lips together, one stitch got caught in between two teeth causing my lip to start bleeding. I made my way into the ladies' toilet, pulled on the light and looked in the mirror, trying very hard not to move my lip. My mouth was full of blood and my top lip was swelling again. When I spoke, the trapped stitch pulled on the thread, making the run of stitches instantly taut and causing my lip to bleed. I spat the blood out of my mouth and rinsed it out with some cold water and then I set about unpicking the knot.

I could hear Sister calling me. I shouted that I was in the ladies and would be out shortly. There was only one thing for it. Reaching into my top pocket I got out my pair of scissors. The thread was hanging out of the left corner of my mouth by a good inch and it looked like I had a whisker, like a cat. I snipped off the thread as close to my lip as possible and then tried to smile in order to get the thread to reverse itself. It did not work, so I got a pin out of my pocket and unpicked as many of the stitches as possible. I managed to unpick about five stitches before coming across another knot. I cut the thread for the second time, and the knot fell into the sink. Sister called again. I cut off the thread, dabbed my mouth and rinsed out the blood that was swishing around inside it. Pressing hard on my lip with some wet tissues, I managed to stem the blood which had trickled down my chin and onto my uniform. A few dabs with the wet tissue removed much of the obvious signs of blood, but left a circular light red stained area. Replacing my bib with a plastic cover I made my way out of the toilet. Sister gave me a funny look, but she did not ask about my lip, even though it had obviously been bleeding.

'Room seven,' she said. 'Someone has pressed the attention bell.'

'Sure, Sister.'

I made my way round to room seven and switched the attention bell off.

'Did someone call?' I asked.

No one moved. No one said a word. When I popped my head inside the curtains round each of the beds, everyone seemed to be asleep. Sister called me to go the side room again. The patient had taken a turn for the worse and her breathing was quite laboured. Her eyes were wide open.

'Constance,' she said, 'help me.'

She had fallen off her pillows and was propped up on her

elbow at the side of her bed. She had a startled look on her face, as though she had seen a duppie. Sister and I got her back sitting upright on her pillows.

'Now, luvvie, is there anything I can get you?' asked Sister.

She shook her head. Sister pulled the oxygen mask back up around her face and within a minute or two she seemed to come alive again.

'That's better, luvvie,' said Sister. 'Now can I get you some painkillers that will help you sleep?'

She nodded and I saw death come into her eyes. They were vacant. Time seemed to leave her eyes and in its place I sensed she saw just grey blue darkness.

'Have something to drink, dear,' said Sister, handing me a beaker of water to give to her.

I tried to feed it to her, but it just seeped out of her mouth. She did not cough, or resist. She just stared ahead with empty eyes. Sister pulled the curtains across the bed and indicated to me to leave the room. The patient was comfortable. She had everything she could possibly need. In her hand she still clutched her rosary, but her Bible had fallen on the floor. I picked it up, placed it on her lap and quietly left the room.

I went to wash my hands and then decided to check room seven again. One of the male patients was stirring uneasily.

'Can I get you anything?' I said.

He opened his eyes. He was in his seventies and had sparse grey hair covering the back half of his head. The rest was shiny hairless skin that fitted around the hair like a skull cap. His arms were under the sheet and counterpane.

'Nurse,' he said in a weak voice.

What's the matter?'

'Nurse,' he repeated.

I moved his bedside table to one side and approached his bed, bending down as close.

'What is the matter? What is it?'

I moved as close to him as I could, in the hope he would tell me what was the matter. As I did so he drew his crinkly hand from underneath the bedclothes, pressed the palm into my face, brushed his hand down the side of my uniform and then grabbed hold of it.

'What's wrong?' I said, trying to break free from his grip.

'Nurse,' he moaned, plaintively and brought his other hand up from under the bedclothes to touch the other side of my face. He was gripping my uniform fiercely.

'Come on,' I said, 'it's not that bad.'

There was an overwhelming stench of something rotten.

'Just a moment.' I switched on the bedside light.

The patient had smeared excrement all over my uniform. It was in my face, mouth, hair and my hands were covered in it. So was the patient, and he still had a large amount in his free hand ready to smear all over me. His other hand was gripping me so tightly that I could not escape, so I pressed the buzzer for help. A nurse ran in and together we forced his hand away. What he had done was disgusting, but it seemed an act of such desperation that he still needed help.

'You have been very naughty,' I said. 'Now just keep still while I try and tidy you up.'

I pulled the covers back and the stench almost knocked me out. He had unpicked his colostomy bag and squeezed out the faecal contents. The bag was between the patient's legs and he had obviously spent some considerable time getting the faeces out. His index and middle fingers were covered up to the hilt, where he had inserted them into the bag to remove final remnants. Sister appeared from behind the curtain and gave the patient a good talking to, which seemed to calm him down. She told me to clean myself up and leave the patient to Nurse.

As I left, I realised the enormity of what he had done. My stitches had not healed as well as I would have liked and there was a real risk of infection. Using some sterile wipes I cleaned my lips thoroughly and then did it twice more before I cleaned my face. I pursed my lips so that the filth would not affect my stitches. Stepping out of my uniform, I put on one of the kitchen orderly's overalls and sluiced mine down. I tried as hard as I could to get the faeces out of my hair with a hot shower hose, but the stench simply would not go away.

When I was done I went back to finish cleaning up the patient. In my pocket I had two pairs of plastic gloves. Sister was behind the curtain and she had started to clean him up. She was definitely on the war path. It was not the first time the patient had collected his faeces and redistributed it among the nursing staff. If he wanted to behave like an animal, we would treat him like an animal. There was absolutely no excuse for his behaviour at all. He lay there, silenced by her sharp tongue. She never raised her voice. She never spoke harshly to the patient, but she left him in no doubt that what he had done was completely out of order. Sister had cleaned him up and replaced his colostomy bag with a new one. The rest of the bedclothes were removed. During all that time, the patient never once said 'Nurse'. Flicking off the light, Sister opened his curtains while I wheeled the dirty linen trolley out of the ward. I would need another wash: I smelt like an old toilet. Sister smelt the same and no amount of perfume helped with the stench.

Just before midnight Sister did a ward check and I went with her. All was quiet in the first seven wards. Most of the patients were asleep or at least quite close to that state. Mr Colostomy Bag was awake, but he looked as though he was thinking about his future. We stepped into the side ward. Sister listened to the lady's breathing. Rather to my surprise, she was still alive. I noticed that the Bible was on the floor again. The patient had her eyes half closed and her hands firmly clasped together as though in prayer. Sister removed the mask, and asked her if she wanted it turned down low for the night, but she did not answer. Her grey-black eyes looked forward into the darkness ahead. Sister touched her forehead, but there was no reaction. Reaching for the patient's wrist, Sister checked her pulse. The patient's head rested gently on the pillows, her hair beautifully laid out round her shoulders, her legs slightly bent at the knees. Sister shook her head. It was no good, she was dead. Sister brought her right hand down over the still face and very gently closed her eyelids.

'I'll call the doctor,' Sister said, 'to confirm time of death.'

The patient looked beautiful, at peace with herself and her Maker. There was no more pain, no more oxygen. The patient had gone where she was happy to go. While Sister was ringing for the doctor, I set about tidying up the body. I removed a bowl from the sluice and filled it with warm soapy water. Collecting three towels on the way back into the room, I made a start on washing the corpse. I placed the bowl on the side trolley and the towels at the bottom of the bed together with a face flannel. I removed all the pillows and placed them on the armchair, before stripping the bed of all sheets save for the undercover bedsheet. I removed the cushions from under the patient's knees so she was now able to lie flat.

'I'm just going to give you a wash,' I said. 'I hope you don't mind. I'll start at the top and work my way down.'

I started with her face, washing and drying as I went along. Then I did her neck and both arms. Then I turned her on to her right side so I could do her left side, back, chest and leg. Having got the patient into a comfortable position, I decided that it would be better to have clean water. I walked to the sink, emptied the water down the sink and gave the bowl a quick rinse. I put some bubble bath in the water. She would be smelling like a rose garden when I had finished.

When I returned, the newly deceased exhaled quite loudly. It was more of an 'aaah.' I heard it loud and clear and it froze me to the spot. I could not move. My gaze was fixed on her and I felt a terror rise from my toes up to my heart. I was convinced that her spirit had left her body and her duppie was in the room. As I stared at her she did it again, this time even louder than before.

'Agggh,' she said and she definitely did say it, because I saw her lips move. At that moment I was paralysed by fright. Then I came round and ran out of the room with my bowl full of soapy water. I bumped into Sister in the hall. She steadied me and slowed me down.

'Are you all right?' she said.

'Sister,' I said, 'she is alive. She made a noise. I heard her myself.'

'No!' said Sister. 'Are you sure?'

'Yes, Sister, I am.'

'She had no pulse when I took it,' said Sister, looking puzzled. 'I'd better check again. Come with me.'

I was reluctant to follow Sister into the room. I stood by the door so that I could make a quick escape if there were a duppie in the room.

'No pulse there,' said the Sister. 'Are you sure she spoke to you?'

'Yes, Sister, I am sure.'

'Well what did she say?'

'She said "agggh" twice.'

'Twice?' queried Sister.

'Yes, on two occasions when I turned my back to get some water.'

'Well, did she say anything else?'

'No just that.'

'Did she move?'

'No.'

Sister started to laugh.

'Constance,' said Sister, 'I think you may find that she is dead and was simply expelling trapped air from her body.'

I felt like a right twit. Sister thought it was quite funny and when the doctor turned up she told him that I had run out of the room when the patient expelled air. He chuckled. Long after the doctor was gone, I continued the bed bath on the patient. Her relatives had been informed and were on their way. The patient did not require any make-up. She looked truly beautiful without it. All her personal property had been itemised and was ready for collection. When the family arrived they stayed for about an hour behind the curtain paying their last respects and then they all left, except a rather good looking young man in his mid thirties. He approached me and asked me if I would be good enough to tell him where Sister was. I found her in room four.

'One of the relatives would like a word,' I said.

'What about?'

'I don't know, but it sounds urgent.'

'Very well, tell him I'll be along in a moment.'

I did so and she was true to her word. She introduced herself and asked what she could do for him.

'Well,' said the young man, and paused as if he were a little embarrassed. 'I was just wondering whether my aunt has left a will.'

'A will!' said Sister. 'I've no idea. Were you expecting one?'

'Well, yes and no. I was just wondering whether my aunt might have mentioned it.'

'I don't think she did,' said Sister, 'but I am not the person to ask. You might want to talk to the day staff or the person in charge of legal affairs.'

He thanked Sister and went back into the side room to pay his last respects to his aunt.

'Sister,' I said, 'is that typical? That members of the family ask about a will before the body is cold?'

Sister laughed.

'Constance, you should not take things so personally. Relatives are entitled to ask about a will. Admittedly it is a bit awkward, but that never stopped a family member before.'

I was heartbroken. As I walked past the side room, the curtains were drawn around the bed. I wondered what the relatives had been doing. I imagined them trying to wake her up to ask her about a will. Well, I wasn't having any of that. She was entitled to die with dignity, without having the family hovering about trying to work out who left what to whom. I went past the door three times trying to see what was going on. I hoped the young man was paying her due respect, but as I walked up past the door for the fourth time Sister asked me what I was doing.

'Nothing,' I said.

'Well in that case the patient in room two needs a bed pan.'

I went off to get on with my duties. I had allowed my imagination to run away with me and that was not good. The rest of the night passed without incident and by the time the day staff came on duty we had lost only one patient during the night. I was exhausted. I arrived at Miss Lindsey's smelling like a sewer. It was a good thing that she was not in. Before I went to bed I washed my uniform ready for the night duty later that day. A hot bath was next. I scrubbed my face and washed my hair. My lips were slightly swollen and red. Cleaning my lips with an antiseptic wipe I checked the shape of my lips in the mirror. They were much reduced in size, but in my eyes they were still hideous.

I woke up in the middle of the night with a bad headache and running a temperature. It was not like me at all, but when the time came to get up and go to work I was not feeling up to it. It was the first time I was not looking forward to going to work. By the time I arrived at Lyndhurst Gardens the fresh air and long walk had made me feel better. The handover report took no time at all and I set about my tasks with only one aim in mind; to get the job done as quickly as possible without a repeat of the night before. By the time Sister was handing out the drugs, I had done the teas, bedpans, kitchen and sluice. I had come over all queer and had to lie down to recover. Nurse asked if I wanted some pills for my headache, but I decided against that. During the night I did not improve and as soon as I boarded the train to Newcastle I fell asleep. I woke up only twenty minutes from my destination. By the time I got to Jesmond Dene all I wanted was my bed and I remained there all next day.

8
Father Battle

Fortunately I had done most of my course work, so I simply had to do a bit more reading. Gradually my temperature fell and my headache disappeared. I decided I was just exhausted. I might have to try to cut down on trips to London. At the start of term I enjoyed meeting Jo and Pauline again. They were a still a good laugh and although J had behaved pretty badly, I still liked him. We resumed being just mates. Most students hated land law, but I found Professor Clark inspiring. His was the first lecture, followed by ones on contract and tort.

In the coffee room in our break we huddled around the window, which had always been our spot. Jo was the first out of the lecture room to bag the chairs. She had spent the holidays earning money. She was such a clever person she had no need to do course work out of term. She was bound to get a First. Alison had spent her time at home with her parents and her sister. She had caught up on a lot of course work during the holiday. I felt that I had not worked hard enough and was getting my priorities all wrong, but I had to eat and pay for my surgery. J had done no work at all, or so he said.

At the end of the day we had a quick drink in the Union. Alison seemed to be getting on quite well with a lad called Kevin. It was clear to me that she liked him, but I thought that she was too shy to do anything about it. She was too much of a lady. I thought about arranging a small dinner or drinks party to help the romance along. It was in the third week of term that we decided to have a dinner party in the flat. We had arranged the seating plan so Alison would sit next to Kevin. The dinner had been agreed for the next Friday so that no one felt under pressure to go home early.

Ever since my strange turn in Lyndhurst Gardens, I had not felt completely well, but things were about to get a lot worse. On Tuesday my temperature rose sharply and I developed a fever. I had pains in my back, my head, legs and every time I moved I felt like I was about to drop. I called in on the porter, who told me to go to sick bay and when nurse examined me she booked me in immediately. My temperature was worryingly high and there was no sensible explanation for it. When I told her that I had had a high temperature on and off for several weeks, nurse became quite alarmed and said that she wanted the doctor to have a look at me. It was several hours before he came and during that time I was monitored hourly. By the time the doctor arrived my temperature was still high. I was given no choice – I had to stay in overnight. I stupidly had not expected this and had not brought my night clothes. Fortunately the porter rang up to find out whether there was any news of me. He was very kind and brought my night things and a few of my books to sick bay.

At about three in the afternoon of that day Father Battle came in to see me. When I first arrived at Newcastle, I had put on my personal information that I was a Catholic and Father Battle had popped in to introduce himself because he might have to pray for me. I had not been to Mass often, but I was still one of his flock. As he came through the door he was everything I thought a Catholic priest should be – tall, slim to medium build and with a gleaming white dog collar around his neck. His face was quite lined from doing God's work and he had creases from just above his temple to way below his mouth. When he smiled, his face folded back on itself to display the most perfect teeth in the world. They were very white and they gleamed at you. I just could not take my eyes off his teeth. I suppose you needed to have good teeth when you were passing on God's message. You had to be able to impress people, get them to listen to you and it helped to have perfect teeth like Father Battle's.

'Hello, I'm Father Battle. Do you mind if I sit down.' He made room for himself on the side of the bed. 'How are you feeling?'

'I'm good, Father.'

'Well you cannot be good if you are in here.'

'Well, I have a high temperature, Father, and they don't know what has caused it.'

'And do you know?'

'Yes I do.'

'What's that? Please don't say if you don't want to.'

'I think God is trying to punish me.'

Father started to laugh and as he threw his head back, his eyes were blue, ice cold blue.

'And why do you say that?'

'Just because, Father.'

'Just because of what?'

'Well, just because I think He has got it in for me.'

He roared, a real belly laugh.

'And how long do you say He's had it in for you?'

'Oh, as long as I can remember, really.'

Father slowly seemed to realise my situation was actually not a laughing matter.

'You believe in God, don't you?' he said.

'Now and then,' I said, 'but if I was not a Catholic I would not believe.'

Father had to think about that one.

'Are you serious that God's got it in for you?'

'I am absolutely sure about it,' I said. 'I used to think that he had got it in just for me. I don't know of a single other person who has had to put up with the kind of special treatment God has dished out to me. I suppose that makes me very special.'

Father was still staring at me when nurse came and took my temperature.

'Constance,' he said, as soon as the nurse had taken the thermometer out of my mouth, 'you sound almost like a non-believer.'

'I think I must be getting quite close to that.'

'And what is it that has brought you to this state of mind'?

'It is a long story, Father.'

'Well, I have the time if you want to talk.'

I thought about this for a moment.

'Well, Father, maybe I don't want to talk about it.'

Father took this in his stride.

'Tell me about you, Constance.'

'What do you want to know?'

'Well, Constance is a very English name. How did you get that?'

'I've only had that name since I left school.'

'School, Constance?'

'Yes.'

'And what is the relevance of school and your name? I don't understand.'

'Well, it was when I was leaving school that I discovered my name was Constance.'

'And you did not know before?'

'No.'

'What was your name before you were Constance?'

'Clare.'

'Tell me a bit about your parents. Let's start with your mother.'

'I don't know that much about my mother.'

'Well, where is she from'?

'I think it is Portland in Jamaica.'

'Portland, you say, and have you been there?'

'No.'

'And do you want to visit one day?'

'No.'

'Not even to see where your mother comes from?'

'No, Father.'

'And why is that, if you don't mind me being personal?'

'Because, Father, I have no wish to visit where she came from, ever.'

'I take it you don't get on with your mother.'

'No I don't, Father.'

'Well that is a pity. you should try and make your peace.'

'I think not, Father.'

'Do you have sisters and brothers?'

'Yes.'

'Tell me, Constance, how many sisters and brothers do you have?'

'Well, that depends on how you count them, Father.'

'Right,' he said, 'this will be interesting. Go on, Constance.'

'Well, I have half brothers and sisters and an adopted sister. There are six Briscoes, which is what I am, four Eastmans, and my adopted sister Denise, who is a Briscoe.

'And are you in touch with them?'

'No, not at the moment.'

Nurse returned to take my temperature again, but it was still up and she thought I may have picked up an infection. Father Battle had made himself comfortable in sick bay and, as we talked about God and me and my family, he eventually jumped up and said that he had been with me for far too long and he had other patients to see. I asked whether they were all Catholics, or was he able to see non-Catholics, but Father just laughed. At the door he turned and asked if he could visit me again.

'Sure,' I said, 'come whenever.'

'I will,' said Father, 'I will.'

With that he disappeared.

For the rest of the day I got woken up almost every hour as nurse popped the thermometer under my tongue or under my arm. I was encouraged to drink lots of water, but even though I got through a few jugs, my temperature remained worryingly high.

I had no idea what might have brought on my illness. Nurse said that it might have been a rampant bacterial infection which was something I had never heard of. Then I remembered the unpleasant experience at Lyndhurst Gardens when a patient had assaulted me with the contents of his colostomy bag. It had to be that. I became quite ill during the night and my temperature went up again and by the time Father Battle returned I was now on half hourly observations. He entered my room and sat in the same chair as before.

'Hello, Constance,' he said, 'are you better?'

'No, I'm not. In fact, Father, as a result of seeing you I am now a lot worse. I'm on half hour watch.'

Father started to laugh again. I did seem to have the ability to amuse him.

'Are you suggesting that a Messenger from God has made you worse, Constance?'

'Well, it's been known to happen,' I said.

'Now Constance,' he went on, 'I think you are a very interesting person. There is something about you that I am not sure about and I mean to get to know you better.'

Father asked a number of questions about my life, but he got nowhere. I told him that there was nothing to tell. He then asked again about my relationship with my mother.

'It does not exist, Father.'

'Is there any particular reason?'

'No, not really. It's just that we never did get on. We are just very different people who don't like each other.'

'You're very matter-of-fact about this relationship, Constance.'

'Probably because that is the way it has always been, Father.'

'I'm intrigued, Constance. What made you study law?'

'I wanted to be a lawyer.'

'And why Newcastle?'

'I wanted to get away from my mother.'

'When was the last time you actually saw your mother?'

'It must be quite a few years now, Father.'

'And do you intend to make your peace with your mother?'

'No.'

'Never?'

'Never.'

'Surely forgiveness is a virtue, and as a Catholic you cannot bear a grudge for the rest of your life.'

'I think I can, Father. It is not a question of bearing a grudge, it's more a question of not liking my mother.'

'And why is that Constance?'

'She is not a very nice person.'

'Can you not find it in your heart to forgive her, no matter what she has done?'

'No, Father, it's too late for all of that.'

'It is very sad Constance.'

'It is.'

'And you will not reflect on your decision of unforgiveness?'

'No, Father, and before you say it, I know that I'm not going to get into Heaven, so it doesn't matter.'

Father started to laugh again and as he laughed there was not a flicker in his eyes. I knew in my heart that he felt sorry for me. How could he not? He was God's Messenger.

'I would like to come and see you again tomorrow,' he said, 'but only if you would like.'

'That would be very nice, Father, shall we say the same time?'

'Yes,' said Father. 'You are a mystery, Constance, and you make me laugh.'

'Well I'm glad that I make you laugh. Tomorrow it is then.'

The next day he just came straight in and sat by the side of my bed. He was a truly attractive Messenger of God. He smiled at me, it was a Godly smile full of peace on earth and goodwill to all men. I smiled back.

'How are you today Constance?'

'I'm fine thanks.'

'I was thinking about you, Constance, and you worry me. You are so angry with the world and God.'

'Well, he's got a lot to answer for.'

'Yes, so you say, but what about forgiveness?'

'What about it, Father?'

'It is good to remember that to forgive is Divine.'

'And if I don't want to be Divine, Father?'

We both started to laugh. Father stayed for about twenty minutes talking to me about this and that – all to do with God and being a better person. When he got up to go he put his hand in his pocket.

'I've brought a present for you.'

He handed a book with a pink and brown cover to me.

'For me?' I said, astonished. 'I have never had a present from a Messenger of God before. I'm speechless. What can I say? Thank you very much.'

'It's called *The Prophet* by Kahlil Gibran.'

I looked inside the front cover and found he had written 'Constance: some little wisdom (hopefully), with love. Tony.' I had never heard of Kahlil Gibran. He was a poet, philosopher and artist born near Mount Lebanon and his work had been compared to Auguste Rodin's and William Blake's. The blurb on the back said that *The Prophet* was about beautiful, liberating thoughts and as such had been described as more beautiful than the writing of Socrates. I hadn't read Socrates either, so the comparison meant nothing to me. I opened the book and read down the page:

'Some of you say, "Joy is greater than sorrow" and others say, "Nay sorrow is the greater." But I say unto you, they are inseparable. Together they come and when one sits alone with you at your board, remember the other is asleep upon your bed.'

Turning back a few pages I came across the most beautiful verse in the world.

'Then Almitra spoke again and said "And what of marriage, Master?" and he answered saying, "You were born together, and together you shall be for evermore.

You shall be together when the white wings of death scatter your days.

But let there be space in your togetherness and let the winds of the heavens dance between you.

Love one another, but make not a bond of love.

Sing and dance together and be joyous, but let each one of you be alone." '

I read the book from cover to cover before I started on my work.

9
Finals

I hoped to get out of sick bay soon. I was falling behind with my work. My contract assignment was still outstanding and I thought that I might as well start identifying the issues.

By late evening Nurse said I could go home the next day and Father Battle came to see me briefly as I was packing up to go home.

'I loved the book,' I told him.

'I knew that you would enjoy it.'

Back at Jesmond Dene I set about tidying my room and making myself a nice cup of tea. After a good night's sleep I was ready to continue my studies and I quickly fell into my old ways at the law department. I went out for a drink with Jo, Pauline Moulder and Alison Day. Alison was still with Kevin. It was not a big event. We did not get drunk or anything like that – just an orange juice for me and a glass of white for Alison and whatever the rest were having. It was good to be with my mates again. I felt good. We all agreed that it was amazing our third year had come round so fast.

I still had to face my perennial problem. I had spent all of my money having my cosmetic problems sorted out and I had no money to live on. As Miss K would say, that was very silly. I decided to economise on food – one meal a day and no sandwiches at lunch time. After the second week of my enforced diet, I started to notice a difference in my clothes. My jeans slid over my hips and at the end of the third week my tits were definitely smaller. That was not good, since they were not all that big in the first place! When Father Battle came to see me he noticed immediately that I was thinner and thought it was because of the illness that I was still battling with. I did not admit that it was in fact a battle with finance.

By the end of term, despite my assurances to Father Battle that I was well, he refused to be convinced, and he continued to visit me throughout the year in my room in Jesmond Dene. I enjoyed his visits. At first I wondered why the good Father Battle would choose to visit me, a sinner in God's eyes, in my room, but it was simply the best place for the two of us to talk about God and my doubts. Father Battle was such a wonderful priest. He always had faith in me and never accepted that he had lost a one-time believer. We discussed parts of the bible, the prophets – particularly Amos – and also Kahlil Gibran. Father Battle's words of wisdom, his calming influence helped me to come to terms with the fact that I would never consider myself normal, because I never would be. I was just me, Constance Briscoe, and what I really needed in my life was peace and an opportunity to come to terms with myself.

Somehow I managed to eke out my grant money. In a way, it was a boon not to be going to Lyndhurst Gardens. I was now in my final year and I needed to work hard to make sure I had no retakes.

One Friday, Alison and I finally held the long postponed dinner party. It was the first I had ever given in my life. We invited all the usual suspects: Jo, Pauline, Kevin of course and a third year student called Paul S whom I quite liked the look of. A few other random men were also invited to give the night a gender balance.

We had bought large cartons of red and white wine, loads of tins of tomato soup (we had opened them in advance and thrown the tins away just in case anyone looked in the bin). The main course was my speciality chicken and rice, and Alison had baked a cake and bought three kinds of smelly cheese and savoury biscuits. The smell of the cheese was dreadful: they were humming a tune when they were put alongside each other!

It was a brilliant night. The guests arranged to arrive together, because they had been out drinking in the Union. I organised the seating plan and put Alison next to Kevin and myself next to Paul. Unfortunately I had no interest in horses, hare coursing or blood sports, so we had nothing in common. He simply did not want to know.

The soup was superb; we added milk, nutmeg and pepper to personalize it. My main course went down well, too. I noticed Kevin and Alison were chatting away and by the time we were onto the cheese, I knew that they would be an item. It was going rather well until the porter turned up at midnight and said that the men had to leave. He refused to go until he had escorted the last male off the premises. It was a joke. It would have been infuriating if it had not been so funny. There we all were, adults, being treated like naughty children. Still, it was a way of getting rid of everyone without having to force them out of the door. Just as Paul was about to leave he turned to Alison and me and said 'That soup, did you make it yourselves?'

We looked at each other.

'Do you mean, did we add the ingredients?'

'Yes,' said Paul 'that is what I mean.'

'Well,' I said 'we definitely added the ingredients.' Alison started to laugh.

'I smell a rat,' said Paul. 'You don't mind if I have a look in the bin?'

He opened the bin but there were no empty tins! Alison had emptied our bin into the main bin before our guests had arrived, so we did not get caught. I only wish I'd known more about hare coursing and blood sports. Our first attempt at entertaining had gone well.

*　　*　　*

One day, as I approached the law department, I saw J looking out of the window. I caught his eye and we smiled at each other. J was still J and I still liked him. 'If only,' I thought. There was no chance, not even a one percent chance, of us ever getting together again.

Not even my latest cosmetic surgery had saved my relationship with J. He could sod off on the personal stakes, but as far as I was concerned he was welcome to be one of the crowd.

During the year I struggled with some of the subjects, particularly public international law and the philosophy of law. The only reason I did international law was because Jo was so enthusiastic about it. I had read *Introduction to International Law*, eighth edition, by J.G. Starke, also M. Akehurst's *Modern Introduction to International Law*, but despite that I still found it difficult.

But I kept at it, so when the exams came I was well prepared and felt I performed reasonably. I was not in Jo's league but I would probably do OK. In the final days of revision my group had done hardly any socialising, because we were all working flat out. The day exams ended there was a giant piss-up. I had never seen so many legless individuals all face down on University of Newcastle property. It continued for a few days, after which a number of students disappeared for a well-earned break. I stayed in my room most of the time. I had nowhere else to go, no home apart from Jesmond Dene. It was quite wonderful to get to know Newcastle. I loved it now that I had time to spare. I went to the flicks, on my own, had a glass of house red on my own in the Uni and I went for a long walk along the banks of the Tyne, ending up back at the law department. I saw Prof. Ellie as he entered the law department. I was sitting in one of the window seats as he came up the stairs and he raised his hand, acknowledging me. Then to my surprise he came into the common room. It was only me and Professor

113

Ellie. He was such a decent and honourable professor. Not bad looking, either.

'Hello, Constance,' he said.

'Hello Professor Elliot.'

'What brings you here?'

'Oh this and that, Professor Elliot. I'm just hanging about until the big day.'

Back in my room there was not much to do apart from waiting for my results. I checked the balance of my account and much to my surprise I was in credit. In fact, I even had money to spare. I had become used to living on nothing and when my grant cheques did arrive, things did not change very much. I remained in rationing mode.

I still wanted to deal with the scar on my face. I had long ago sought medical advice on how best to remove it, but because of its location and prominence it was difficult to persuade the doctor to scrub my scar away. He said that he was not prepared to take the risk. I dialled the number of his Harley Street clinic. I told them my name, Constance Briscoe, and said I wanted to talk to the doctor. He was on the phone in no time.

'Hello, Constance.'

'Hello, doctor.'

'It's good to hear from you.'

'And you too, doctor.'

'Are you a lawyer yet?'

'Not yet, doctor. I've another year to go at Bar School plus a year's pupillage, but I am getting there.'

We exchanged more superficial pleasantries and then he asked the question I was waiting for.

'What can I do for you, Constance?'

I told the doctor I was worried about my scars and he laughed. Why did everyone always laugh at me?

'Constance you have been worried about those for a good few years now.'

'Do you think you could make them go away, doctor?'

'I don't know, Constance. We have had this discussion a hundred times. It would be a high risk operation and I don't advise it.' There was a long pause. 'Having said that, Constance, I do think that you should consider having your eyes done.'

'My eyes?'

'Yes, your eyes, Constance. It was clear to me last time I saw you that you had deposits of fatty tissue under your eyes which give the appearance of you having bags there. Now that you have had your nose and mouth done they will be more obvious.'

'Constance Briscoe has baggy eyes!' I repeated it. 'I have baggy eyes.'

'I'm sorry, Constance, for being so blunt, but if you really want to improve your appearance then maybe you should consider a reduction or removal of the fatty deposits below your eyes.'

There was an almighty silence and then I said to the doctor:

'Doctor, is there anything else that you think I need?'

'Yes,' said the doctor, 'your teeth stick out and if you had the money and the time we could break your jaw and push your teeth back and then we could reset your jawline.'

'Doctor, you want to break my jaw?'

'Constance, we are in the realm of unnecessary surgery, but that would have a cosmetic effect.'

'But do you want to break my jaw?'

'No, Constance,' said the doctor, 'I do not want to break your jaw and, as I am sure you know yourself, breaking someone's jaw is a criminal offence.'

We both started to laugh.

I arranged to go and see him about my scars and my bags. Before I terminated the call, I told him I was strapped for cash and he laughed and said he had heard it all before. There was nothing to stop me so I went down to London two days later. Whilst I was more concerned about the scars on my face and wanted the doctor to use a cosmetic Brillo pad to get rid of them, he was adamant that my bags were more of a problem and, having looked in the mirror, I agreed with him. We looked at his photographs of me together.

'It is hereditary,' he said. 'You must have got it from your father or mother.'

I thought about it. It was a defect which I definitely did not get from my father's side of the family. The doctor assured me it was not a serious operation – I would not even need to stay in hospital overnight. He would simply scoop out the fat below my eye sockets and, although there would be quite a significant amount of swelling, after four or five days it would subside and eventually I would be left with bag-free eyes.

We discussed the price of the operation and whilst the doctor was reluctant to get immersed in figures, I pressed him and eventually he agreed a price that I could afford. I think I got a reduction on the basis that I had been to his consulting rooms again and again and again. The doctor had given me an appointment in just a week's time. As ever he did a brilliant job. The day after surgery he came to tell me so. I tried to look at him, but my eyes were barely open and it was difficult to focus on anything apart from his white coat and his hand. By 5 pm the same day, I was ready to leave. My dark Rayban sun glasses covered the tell tale signs of my eye operation. As the doctor had promised, the swelling went down and I was very pleased with the results.

As I was recuperating my mind wandered to the future. How would I manage the final leg in my desire to become a barrister? As a result of my status as an independent adult, I qualified for a full grant, thank goodness. As the date came for the publication of the results of my final examinations at Newcastle, I was not nervous. I had worked hard, and I was confident I had passed. In fact all of our group passed. The only person who did exceptionally well was Jo. She got a First and she deserved it. The lecturers made themselves available to talk through any problem that the students might have, but I did not have any problems. I was relieved, like all the other students, that it was all over. Professor Clark, Professor Elliott and a whole host of other lecturers congratulated us and had a glass of wine with us. The wine was in two cardboard boxes, which were lined with an inner plastic belly, with a spout which was joined to the plastic belly but protruded beyond the outer cardboard. There were plastic glasses. We had a choice of red or white. I was standing in the corner talking about inconsequential things when Professor Elliott approached our group.

'Miss Briscoe,' he said, 'are you enjoying the wine?'

It was not too bad, considering, and I did prefer the red to the white so I told him so.

'Miss Briscoe,' he said, 'when you first arrived here we had a similar conversation and you mentioned that you did not drink.'

'Did I?' I said, 'I don't remember that. Anyway I don't much.'

'No, but I *do* remember, Miss Briscoe, and I said then what I'm about to say again now.'

'What's that, Professor Elliott?'

'See me again in three years' time. I am glad to see that you have proved my theory correct.'

'What theory, Professor Elliott?'

'That there is an inconsistency in reading law for three years and not drinking alcohol.'

I laughed, as did he. He congratulated me on my degree and moved on.

We were all due to graduate in a couple of days' time and there was much talk among the students about graduation day. It was obvious to me that I could not attend. My parents would not turn up to have their photographs taken with me. My mother I had long ago refused to speak to and I hadn't seen her in years. My father, well he might come along if he was not busy doing other things, but I wasn't going to tell either of them. I didn't know anyone else who could be stand-in parents.

Imagine the embarrassment when the photographer asked for my parents to join me in the photograph and no one stepped forward! The only way to avoid that situation was not to attend my graduation day.

After all the wine was drunk and the used plastic cups crushed, I said goodbye to my mates, including J, and we promised to keep in touch. For the final time I made my way to my room and packed my things to be sent back to London. My last night in my room was not easy. The cheap alcohol was affecting my head and twice I woke up only to realise that it was not morning. Just when I went back to sleep the second time, I found that Miss K was in my head. She was not sad, she was happy. She was in her twinset, clapping and smiling. 'See,' she said, 'see' and then she was gone. The next day I handed my keys in at the porter's lodge and left Jesmond Dene for good. I bought a one-way ticket back to London.

Back in London I arranged to stay with my friend Jeffrey. When I was about fifteen I was working in a restaurant in the holidays and he came in for a meal. He was at least twenty-five years older than me and had become a friend, even a father figure. He had children my age. He was divorced and lived in a very spacious two bedroom flat. He did not mind me staying with him as long as I kept out of the way when his girlfriends were about. He was a property developer and very generous to me. With hindsight he might have come up to my graduation if I had thought to invite him. A few days after graduation day, I received a letter from Professor Clark. He was very annoyed. He made it clear that I should have attended my graduation. We were all students together and we should have all graduated together. That was how he put it. I called him and apologised. I made an excuse which he just about found acceptable. I did not have the heart to tell Professor Clark that the real reason was my lack of parents. I agreed that I would stay in touch with him and keep him apprised as I made my way through life.

Two weeks post graduation I got my graduation certificate and I was mighty proud, even though I had no one to show it to, so I kept it under my mattress in the envelope. That was the best way to keep it flat and there was no chance of it getting wet. I had stopped wetting the bed long ago. The name on my certificate was Constance Briscoe.

In the course of my final year, I had been surprised to receive a letter from a firm of solicitors enquiring if I was Nurse Clare. I wrote back and confirmed that I was. They wrote by return to tell me that a lady called Mrs Rol had left me a bequest in her will. I remembered her. She had been a patient at St George's Hospital in Tooting when I was an auxiliary nurse. There were a number of unresolved issues. The lawyers would deal with those. In the meantime I moved, two weeks before I started to study for my Bar exams, into 39 Tremadoc Road, Clapham. It was in a right state when I got it but my father was handy with his tools. It was a house that I would eventually own, but meanwhile it was at a very reasonable rent, and only a few miles from where I was brought up in Camberwell. It was a large house and I planned to let rooms out to other students at the Council of Legal Education. For the first time in my life I would have an income without working my backside off.

In September I travelled by underground from Clapham South to Chancery Lane to start my Bar course. We were taught how to write a legal opinion. We practised dozens of opinions and did lots of advocacy exercises. That was the bit I liked best. My mother could have given me an excellent reference for arguing and those skills I could bring to bear as an advocate. The academic options I had chosen were crime, evidence, family and revenue law. In addition to that I had to study two general papers. It was hard work. When the course was over I revised methodically. The right questions came up in the final examinations. I passed and had finished exams for ever. Hurrah! All that was left was to finish eating my dinners in the Temple. Even though I was a member of Inner Temple I did not make one single friend. It is a place where many students simply pass through.

For hundreds of years barristers have worked in the four Inns of Court close to the Law Courts in the Strand. They are like legal colleges with dining halls and a library, around which the barristers' chambers are grouped. In olden times the students lived with their pupilmasters in the Inns and were taught advocacy and law after dinner in Hall. It is the Treasurer or head of the Inn who calls you to the Bar. Before that a student still has to eat his or her dinners. I was supposed to have consumed twenty-one such meals, but as it was expensive to travel down from Newcastle, I had not eaten any. My Inn was Inner Temple. I had chosen it because Gandhi had been a member there. I called the Inner Temple office and booked twenty-one dinners. For three weeks solid I ate my way through a lot of indifferent food. Most of the other students were intent on drinking as much as they could, particularly the port provided after dinner. When I had finished I informed the Student Advisor that I was now ready to be called to the Bar. On November 22, 1985, I made my way to Inner Temple Hall, dressed up for the first time in my wig, black gown and collarette with starched white bands and waited in a line with the other students. Although my parents were not present, there were so many people milling around that they could have been somewhere in the hall. I did stand out though, as one of the few black faces. My name was called out and I walked up to the Treasurer who said: 'Constance Beverley Briscoe I call you to the degree of the Utter Bar. Well done.' He shook my hand. At long last I was called to the Bar. Constance, formerly Clare, formerly Clearie Briscoe. I knew Miss K was applauding me somewhere. I slipped out of the Hall early and made my way back to Tremadoc Road. It was time to write again to Mike Mansfield.

10
Trouble

1984

I was now at the very point I had wanted to be when I first met Mike Mansfield, all those years ago on a school visit to Knightsbridge Crown Court. Nothing could stop me becoming a real barrister, not just like the actors who had inspired me on television. Picking up my pen, I set about composing the last letter I would ever write to Mr Mansfield with regard to my pupillage. It was eight years since he had agreed to be my pupilmaster – to train me for twelve months. I looked forward to my master's trade. I relished this moment. Clearie, Clare, Constance was on her way.

> July 1984

> Dear Mr Mansfield
>   I am sorry for the delay in contacting you, but I thought that you would like to know that I have just passed my exams at the College of Legal Education. I am going to have a bit of a break and then I would like to start pupillage at a time convenient to you. It would be good if we could meet up and just have a chat about my pupillage.
>   I look forward to hearing from you at your earliest convenience.

He had obviously gone on holiday, because I did not get an immediate reply. When the letter eventually arrived, I recognised his big bold writing immediately. It was a short note.

September 8, 1984

Dear Constance
    Come as soon as you like.
    Michael

I read his note over and over again. He said 'Come as soon as you like.' As soon as I liked – get that! Tapping in the telephone number, I waited for the clerk to Michael Mansfield to answer the phone.

'May I help you?' said the voice at the other end of the line.

'May I please speak with Mr Michael Mansfield?'

'And who shall I say is calling?'

'Miss Briscoe, Miss Constance Briscoe.'

'And what is it regarding?'

'It's private,' I said, not knowing what else to say.

'Will you just wait a moment?' said the voice.

'Sure.'

The line went dead for a few moments and then he returned.

'I'm very sorry, Miss Briscoe, but Mr Mansfield is no longer a member of these Chambers.'

'What does that mean?'

'Mr Mansfield has left these Chambers.'

'Left these Chambers?' I said, 'But when?'

'Quite recently, Miss Briscoe.'

'May I know a number where I can contact him?'

'I'm afraid we don't give out telephone numbers.'

'But I have to get in touch with him.'

'Well, there's nothing I can do about that.'

'But he is expecting my call.'

'Again, madam, I'm not sure that I can take that into account.'

Mike Mansfield was gone and I did not know where to find him. Why hadn't he told me in his letter?

The phone went dead. I was in shock. I had to get hold of Mike Mansfield.

I sat down and had a cup of tea. He would not have gone too far, I was sure. I suddenly had a searing headache and my hand was shaking. The best thing was to leave it overnight and think about it tomorrow when things were clearer in my mind. I went to bed, but could not get to sleep. I kept hearing that voice – 'I'm sorry, Miss Briscoe, but Mr Mansfield is no longer in these Chambers.'

The next morning my head had cleared and I had a solution. I went to the library and located the Bar Directory, which names every member of the Bar and gives details of their speciality and where they could be contacted in Chambers. Mike Mansfield was indeed in the Bar Directory, but the details that were provided for him were his former Chambers in Cloisters. It was obviously out of date.

Back home I lay on my four poster bed with the curtains drawn thinking about my options. They were diminishing by the minute. How could Mike Mansfield just leave Chambers and not tell me? It did not make sense. He would not just up and go and leave me without a pupillage. I fell asleep. I was tired from the night before and when I woke up this time it was late morning or early afternoon. I reached for the phone again and tapped in the Cloisters number. A different voice answered: young, definitely Essex boy.

'May I help you?'

'Yes, I'm trying to get in touch with Mr Michael Mansfield.'

'And who shall I say is calling?'

'Miss Briscoe. I am due to start a pupillage with him and I'm having trouble getting in touch with him.'

'And what number do you have?'

'Well, just this one really. I've always contacted him on this number.'

'Miss Briscoe, Mr Mansfield left these Chambers recently.'

'Well, do you have a contact number for him?'

'Yes, we do, but we have a policy of not giving out the details.'

'Well, would it be possible for you to contact him and give him my details?'

'I'm afraid that is not possible, Miss Briscoe.'

'Well, what am I supposed to do?'

'Miss Briscoe, I'm afraid I cannot advise you.'

'And you are sure you cannot pass a message to him?'

'I'm quite certain, Miss Briscoe. I'm sorry I cannot help.'

What was I to do? So much for 'come any time.' Did I need this? No. I had a feeling that I had to turn detective to hunt Mike Mansfield down.

It was now two o'clock. I would go to his old Chambers and demand to know his whereabouts. If I hurried I could be there by four. I tidied myself up, tied my hair back and put on some make-up. I bought a ticket from Clapham North Station to Chancery Lane. I knew how to get there from days of eating dinners in Inner Temple Hall. I had to turn left out of Chancery Lane Station and then first left again down Chancery Lane until I came to a jewellery shop called Attenboroughs on the corner with Fleet Street. I crossed over the road and made my way through a vast door with a stone lamb on top, and into Middle Temple Lane. At Brick Court I turned left into Pump Court and came to Cloisters. The Chambers were in the far right-hand corner. Outside on the wall was a list of names of the barristers who had tenancies there.

Barristers in independent practice are self-employed, but take tenancies in Chambers that provide the kind of practice they want to offer. The clerks act for all the barristers. When you have completed your pupillage, you hope to be offered a tenancy in your pupillage chambers. It is the most important moment in a young barrister's career.

Michael Mansfield's name was still on the board near the top. Had they been fooling me? Did he not want to give me a pupillage after all? My courage ebbed away. I sat on a step at the bottom of the stairs and wondered what to do. I had not actually thought about that. I could not exactly go into

Chambers. What if the voice recognised me? That would never do. There was only one thing for it – I had to wait. If he was still there, this was about the time he would come back to Chambers after court. I sat down on the bottom step. There was no point in wasting time. I got my novel out and made myself comfortable. With my back to the list of names I brought my knees up to my chin and settled down with my book. If Mike returned there was no way that he could pass me without my seeing him.

My book was completely fascinating and I read at least ten pages before the first person stepped over me. It was not exactly a dirty look, but I got the distinct impression that I should not have been there and I was a bit of an eyesore. No one said a word to me in the first couple of hours, but then Essex boy came down the stairs: I recognised his voice as soon as he spoke. He quite deliberately stepped over me when all he had to do was walk round my legs. Stepping over me must have been intended to invade my personal space. He turned to face me.

'May I help you?' he said.

I ignored him. He could not be talking to me, because I had rung up twice now and apparently no one was in a position to help me.

'Can I help you?' he said again.

I looked up. There was something familar about him. There was nothing memorable about his face. It was bland, nothing special – in fact I cannot even remember the colour of his hair. What I do remember is the suit – well it was not a suit, it was in fact a pair of trousers, shirt and tie, but I got the impression that the trousers were part of a suit. It was blue black, with a faint stripe in grey. It was a sharp suit, but there was still something odd about him. I found myself staring between his legs when he said again:

'Can I help you?'

'No,' I said. 'Thank you.'

Suddenly I got it: it was his legs – I had seen them before:

'Can I help you, madam?' he said with emphasis and a trace of sarcasm.

'No you cannot help me,' I said, just as emphatically.

I knew where I had seen those legs before. It was in a John Wayne movie, many years ago. His legs were bowed. It was at its most obvious at the knees where the gap was largest. It was a sort of diamond shaped space between his legs. From where I was sitting, I had a clear view through the diamond and back to the Cloisters. It was so peaceful, so beautiful. It was the most beautiful and enchanting view I had ever had between the legs of an Essex man.

'Miss,' he said, 'I've got to tell you that you cannot stay here.'

'I am so sorry,' I said, 'I thought you were talking to someone else. I'm fine thanks. I don't need any help.'

He seemed rather irritated, or was it impatient? As I stared between his legs I counted nine people coming and going. Six men and three women. The sun was shining.

'It's a glorious day,' I said, trying to lighten the conversation, but he was having none of it.

'You have to move on,' he said.

'I have to what?' I said, as a man in a black pin stripe trousers passed from left to right across the gap between his legs.

'Move on, Miss, you cannot stay here.'

'I have no intention of staying here, sir,' I said.

'I don't mean to be offensive, Miss, but can I take it that you will move on?'

'Certainly not, no.'

'Why are you here, Miss? What do you want?'

'I'm waiting for Mr Michael Mansfield.'

'And what business do you have with Mr Mansfield?'

'It's private.'

'Well, Miss, I can tell you that Mr Mansfield is no longer here.'

'I know that,' I said. 'I rang up yesterday and was told.'

'What's your name, Miss?'

'Constance Briscoe, Miss Constance Briscoe.'

'I remember, it was me you spoke to.'

'In fact, I rang twice the day before,' I said.

'Ain't you got a pupillage with Mr Mansfield, Miss?'

'Yes, that's right.'

'Mr Mansfield has set up a new set of Chambers.'

'A new set of Chambers?'

'It's more than my life is worth to have told you.'

'And what set is that?' I said.

'I can't remember the exact title, Miss, but I think it is Tooks Court.'

'Where is that?'

'I don't know. Now, will you please move on, Miss?'

'Why should I?' I said defiantly.

'Miss, we'll be in serious difficulties come four thirty!'

'And what's so special about four thirty?' I asked.

'Well, Miss, that's when the three conferences are booked in. We've got lots of people coming, clients and solicitors and all, and the Head of Chambers is just not going to allow a situation where they are stepping over you. So will you please be good enough to pack up and move on.'

'I really meant to cause no offence,' I said.

'Likewise, Miss, now will you please move on?'

'Where is Tooks Court?' I said.

'Miss, search me. I've gone out of my way to help you. Please go.'

'What if this is just an attempt to get rid of me?'

'What?'

'This story about a new set of Chambers could be all cock and bull.' He looked sweet, in his dazed Essex-boy best.

'If you don't believe me, ring the Bar Council, they have details of everyone at the Bar.'

'And how do I get hold of their number?'

'Try the telephone directory, Miss.'

That was a good idea, I thought they must know where he is.

'Will you go now, Miss?'

I got up, brushed my knees with my hand and swept my bottom with a series of backhanded swipes.

'I think I will. Thank you. You've been very helpful.'

'It's a pleasure, Miss. I hope you find Mr Mansfield.'

Putting my book away, I made my way past Middle Temple Hall and up Chancery Lane to the underground station. As I walked along I had another idea. Some years ago I had written to another barrister called Henry Pownall to ask for his help in finding Chambers. He would know where Mike had moved to.

When I got home, I found Mr Pownall's number in an old address book and early next morning I called him. His clerk answered and enquired who wanted him.

'Miss Briscoe.'

'Just a moment, Miss Briscoe.'

In less than a minute he was on the phone.

'Now,' he said, 'It's Constance Briscoe, is that right?' He seemed to remember me. 'How are you, my dear?'

'I'm good, thank you.'

'And what can I do for you?'

'Well, Mr Pownall . . .'

'Henry, please,' he said. 'Call me Henry.'

'Henry, I'm trying to get hold of Michael Mansfield to arrange a date to start my pupillage, but I don't seem to be able to find him and his former Chambers have told me that he recently left. I was just wondering whether you can help?'

'That's right, Constance, Michael Mansfield has left his Chambers and if I'm not very much mistaken he has set up Tooks Court Chambers.'

'Do you have a number for Tooks Court Chambers?'

'No, but I'm sure I can get it for you. Just hold on a moment.'

I was put on hold. A few minutes later he was back on the line, giving me the number and address. 'Anything else I can do?'

'No, thank you very much.'

'Well, good luck and do keep me informed. If you need any more help do ring.'

I thanked him and ended the call. I tapped in the number he gave me.

'Tooks Court,' said the voice.

'May I speak with Mr Mansfield?'

'What is your name?'

'Constance Briscoe.'

'Is he expecting your call?'

'Yes and no. I'm trying to arrange my pupillage with him.'

'You have to apply to our Pupillage Committee for that.'

'Yes, but he has already told me I can be his pupil.'

'Has he? Just a moment.' After the moment the voice returned. 'Miss Briscoe, I'm just putting you through to Mr Mansfield.'

'Hello Constance,' said Mike. 'You managed to find me.'

'Yes.' No thanks to you, I thought.

'And I expect you're wondering when you can start your pupillage?'

'Yes I am.'

'Come as soon as you like,' he said.

11

A Cup of Tea and a Biscuit

On Monday November 29, 1984 I got up early to prepare for the start of my pupillage. As I brushed my teeth I caught a good view of my face in the mirror. Not good. I still had to do something about the scars. They were too obvious. My nose and mouth were not bad these days. My skin was in good condition and the shape of my eyebrows was good. I had washed my hair the day before and considering everything I did not look too bad. Once my make-up was on I got into my suit and shirt. I thought I looked the business – professional and tidy, well presented. Picking up my keys, I let myself out, double locking the doors. I made my way to 14 Tooks Court.

Later I was told Mike Mansfield had set up Tooks Court with the aim of achieving equality and fairness for all tenants, regardless of colour or gender. Cloisters had a long standing reputation as a left wing set, but Tooks Court aimed to be even more radical. Some of the senior barristers were well known for their left wing views. It appeared they had been as good as their word, for the three most junior tenants were black women. This looked like the place for me.

I arrived at Tooks Court at a quarter past nine. The clerks were expecting me and one of them showed me up to Mike Mansfield's room, which was the next floor up. Mike had left instructions for me and I was given a brief to read and familiarise myself with until he returned. Mike's room was tiny for such an important barrister. He had a miniature desk, the kind you would get if you were at school. There were three desks in the room, two back to back as you entered the room and another that was just under the window.

'It's a bit tight in here, Miss,' said the clerk who showed me up, 'but it's a new set of Chambers and we are hoping for more space eventually.' The desk that I was to occupy faced Mike's, but whereas I looked out towards the door, Mike faced the window. The other desk, although it was under the window, faced the wall, which was to my right. There was a rack of briefs along the wall, all tied with pink ribbon. Some of them were huge; they went on and on. Some had three or four lever – arch files. I wondered how anyone could master so much material. The clerk searched for a brief and pulled it off the rack. 'Here it is, Miss,' he said. 'This is the brief Mr Mansfield wants you to read.' He disappeared back down the stairs and I settled myself in the room.

There was another person who shared the room with Mike. Her briefs were on the rack closer to the window. The name on them was Janet Plange and looking at the briefs I concluded that she practised in family law. There were a number of other rooms on our landing, a toilet and an area for making coffee. The Chambers were quite small – there were about fifteen members in total. At lunch time I went out to get myself a cup of tea and a sandwich.

It was late in the afternoon when my room mate turned up. I stood up as she entered the room, talking to herself.

'Oh and who have we got here?' she said.

'My name is Constance Briscoe.'

'And mine is Janet Plange.'

'I'm pleased to meet you, Miss Plange.'

'We don't say Mr and certainly not Miss. Call me Janet.' We both sat down at our desks to get on with our work. 'You're Mike Mansfield's new pupil, aren't you?'

'Yes, I am.'

'I had an idea you were coming but I didn't know when. I'm in charge of the pupillage applications and I have to say you've upset one or two people around here.'

I was shocked to hear this. I had only just started at Chambers.

'Did you say I have upset a number of people?'

'Well, there is only one Constance Briscoe around here,' she said.

'How have I upset them?' I said, astonished.

'I seem to remember that you weren't interviewed for a pupillage.'

'Yes, that is correct.'

'And you were not seen by any member of Chambers.'

'I have been writing to Mr Mansfield for years.'

'We have a strict and fair selection process in these Chambers.'

'Really?'

'Yes, really, but you slipped through the net.'

'I don't think I slipped through a net,' I said, defending myself. 'I arranged my pupillage with Michael Mansfield a long time ago.'

'That was in his old Chambers. It's different here.'

There was not much I could say to that. I turned round and tried to concentrate on my work.

'Constance Briscoe,' she said, 'is it really Constance Briscoe?

'Yes,' I said, 'it is.'

'Where did you get that name from? It's a bit posh isn't it? Very English.'

'Do you think so?' I said. 'I don't think it is posh at all.'

'Well, when I received the letter saying we had a Constance Briscoe starting in these Chambers, I very nearly threw it in the bin. It's a good job for you I didn't.'

I wondered whether Janet Plange was one of those who were upset with me, but I decided that it was silly even to consider it. I had as a result of planning secured a pupillage that one or two people were a bit upset about. There was not much I could do about that.

'What university did you go to?' she said.

'Newcastle University,' I said.

'Oh,' she said, 'a proper one. We should have expected that from someone calling herself Constance Briscoe.'

It wasn't long before we were joined by another tenant, Sandra Grayham. I heard her before I actually saw her. When she eventually came up the stairs she exactly fitted the image I had in my mind. When she spoke I recognised a slight West Indian accent. It turned out her family came from Jamaica. She was short, about five feet two inches and stocky – maybe a bit overweight. She had no waist and a large bottom. Her nose was small, flat and bulbous and she styled her hair in a curly perm. She arrived in the room with a large bag on her shoulder and another by her side. I came to know these as her stock in trade. She had on a pleated black skirt and polo neck jumper and a black jacket.

'Ooh, me feet are killing me,' she said as she entered the room and then looking at me, 'Who is this?'

'I'm Constance Briscoe,' I said, standing up.

'Oh hello,' she said. 'You're Mike Mansfield's pupil. Well you can start by making me a cup of tea. One sugar . . . Janet, do you want a cuppa?'

'I wouldn't say no.'

'Two teas, one with sugar, one without, and you can bring mine to my room.' She turned and left the room, turning right. I stood up to go and make the tea when Janet handed me her cup.

'I'll have my tea in here,' she said. 'And make sure you give my cup an extra clean. You can't be too careful in this place.'

I took Sandra's tea to her. She was seated at her desk. There was no one else about, but she clearly shared the room with others.

'Put it there,' she said, creating a space on her desk. I did as I was asked.

'And close the door on your way out.'

Again I did as I was asked. Janet already had a space on her desk for her tea. Reaching up she got hold of a biscuit tin.

'Can you please ask Sandra if she would like a biscuit?' I got up again and went next door.

'Janet would like to know whether you would like a biscuit?'

'I'm watching my weight,' said Sandra. 'Ask her what ones she has got.' I went back into our room.

'Sandra wants to know what ones have you got?'

'Cookies from Sainsbury's,' said Janet Plange.

I took the message back to Sandra.

'Ask her if I can have a look.'

'Can Sandra have a look at the biscuits?'

Janet handed me the tin. I took it to Sandra who chose a biscuit and handed me back the tin.

'Tell Janet I said thank you.'

Returning to the room I handed Janet the tin. I had only just got settled when Sandra said her tea was cold and that she would like another cup, which of course I made. After that I resumed my work.

'Make yourself a cup of tea if you want it,' said Janet Plange.

'No thanks, Janet.'

Almost immediately Sandra came back and exchanged the gossip of the day with Janet. It seemed to be mainly about the dreadful judges that they had appeared before. At about five o'clock Christiana Hyde turned up. She shared a room with Sandra.

'Constance,' said Janet Plange, 'I think more tea is in order. Christiana, do you want a cup of cha?'

'Yes please,' said Christiana.

'Two cups,' said Janet.

'Make that three,' said Sandra.

'Three cups it is,' I said and went off to put the kettle on.

Mike turned up later. He was too busy to talk, having a number of conferences with an instructing solicitor. Because I was not up to speed with the cases, Mike said I did not have to attend the conferences if I did not want to. I decided that I wanted to.

'How is your first day?' Mike asked.

'We've been looking after her while you've not been here, Mike,' said Janet Plange. 'We've kept her busy.'

The conference was due to be held in one of the larger rooms downstairs. I packed up my file and followed Mike. During the conference I kept a note of all that was said and handed it to Mike at the conclusion. I was now free to go home. Twelve more months to go less one day. The clerk had told me they liked to treat their pupils fairly, but I was wondering about that. Pupils were apparently entitled to attend all Chambers meetings although not to vote. This was quite a radical departure from other sets of Chambers where pupils were not allowed to attend any meetings at all and were treated quite badly in comparison.

For the rest of the week I did my very best to keep out of everyone's way. If any member of Chambers wanted assistance, I readily made myself available to do research. There was quite a lot of activity in Chambers. Arthur Scargill, President of the Miners' Union, was squaring up to Margaret Thatcher and it was clear that there would be a strike. Neither was in a mood to back down and worse was to come. A left wing set like ours might attract the work. Two miners had been charged with murdering a taxi driver and I was told the brief was bound to land on Mike's desk. Mike really had very little time to give me guidance, but I did not mind because his cases were so fascinating. Some required a great deal of legal research, which he would do himself. I would prepare them on my own and then compare them with his work.

There was a whole spate of cases concerning miners going through the Courts in Sheffield and Tooks Court Chambers were heavily involved in most of them. Mike was due to defend some miners, who had been charged with riot and unlawful assembly. Because I was his pupil I was given the option of travelling up to Sheffield and finding free accommodation up there. I was offered a room by a solicitor from Sheffield called Mike McColgan. He was a former academic at Sheffield University and had a daughter about my age. The accommodation was Monday to Friday, when I would travel back to London.

Mike McColgan was very kind to me and in return I tried to repay him by cooking my speciality. I cooked rice and chicken every night until he told me that he was sick of chicken and rice and did I know any other dishes. I did not really, so after that Mike cooked for both of us. The miners were having a hard time – in one day alone eighty one miners had been arrested – and it looked as if it was going to get worse. The Chairman of the National Coal Board, Ian McGregor, had announced plans to cut production, the equivalent of twenty pits or twenty thousand jobs. Arthur Scargill had called on the miners to strike, but he refused to hold a ballot.

On December 14 Mike Mansfield and I travelled to a Magistrates Court 'up North'. Mike was due to represent Arthur Scargill himself. He had been charged with two counts of obstruction and had entered pleas of not guilty on an earlier occasion. When we arrived, the press were swarming around. Mike advised me not to talk to the press, in fact not to talk to anyone. In court the press gallery was full to bursting and there was barely enough space for me. I sat behind Mike out of the way. I was terrified that I might do or say the wrong thing. I did not want to cause any problems with my pupillage and hoped that at the end of my pupillage I would be invited to remain at Tooks Court as a permanent member. Mr Scargill seemed completely confident and spoke briefly to the press outside before coming and having a word with Mike. The prosecutor was pretty unsympathetic. He was a bigwig, an important senior barrister. Normally for a charge of obstructing the police you would never get counsel of his or Mike Mansfield's seniority. It was, in fact, the type of charge that I might be expected to defend once I was qualified.

The Magistrate came into court. The defendant was identified and the prosecutor opened the case against him. The Magistrate was told that Arthur had been arrested as he led a large number of pickets to the mine on the fifth consecutive day of the strike. Arthur Scargill tried to stop miners along the path to persuade them not to break the picket, but the police had insisted that the picket kept on the move. A video showed that Mr Scargill had resisted and, when he was told to move on, resisted again, at which point he had been arrested and charged with obstruction.

Mike cross examined and he was brilliant. He argued that the whole scuffle, if that is what it was, had only lasted eighteen seconds. You could time that from the video; the police account that it had lasted much longer simply was not true. Mike suggested that the video demonstrated a preconceived police strategy to move the miners on and remove the leader by arresting him. The police witnesses were not having any of it and argued that their actions were lawful. The Magistrate took no time at all to find Arthur Scargill guilty on both counts of obstruction. He was fined and ordered to pay costs. Outside Court Arthur Scargill was defiant – he told the waiting press that he intended to appeal and that he was not guilty. This was brilliant. Next day the case was in all the newspapers. This was the kind of work I wanted for myself.

For the first six months of pupillage, you are not allowed to do cases yourself in court, but Mike's were so interesting that the time flew by. We spent most of that term in Sheffield. As the Christmas vacation approached I returned to Chambers. My first day back in the room at the top, I came across Janet Plange.

'Hello Constance.'

'Hello Janet.' I unpacked my bag without any additional talk. 'Constance, would you please be good enough to make me a cup of tea?'

'Sure,' I said. I really did not have any objection at all to making tea.

'Now, Constance, you've been in Sheffield, is that right?'

'Yes I have, I've been covering the miners' strike.'

'And who is paying for all of this?'

'I've no idea, Janet.'

'Well, who is paying your fares?'

'I am.'

'How can you afford that?'

'I cannot afford it, but I manage.'

'Oh, we can't have you paying your own fares Constance.'

I assured Janet Plange that I did not wish to have any assistance at all, but she would not hear of it. All pupils had to apply for funding to cover the cost of the fares. It was Chambers' policy. She would mention it to Mike. The matter would be raised in the first Chambers' meeting in the New Year.

Meanwhile Mike had a conference with another Mike, Mike Fisher. I attended the conference and as usual took a note of all that was said and at the end of the conference made a copy for the two Mikes. Mike Fisher smiled at me and I smiled back. He had quite a nice smile. Mike was a partner in a firm called Fisher and Meredith in South London. As I packed up my papers Mike Fisher said:

'And who is the new lady?'

'Oh, I'm sorry,' said Mike Mansfield. 'I thought I had introduced her. Mike Fisher, this is Constance Briscoe, my pupil.'

'Hi,' I said as I packed my bags and bade my leave. I was on my way up stairs when Mike Mansfield called me back.

'Constance, Mike is having his annual end of year Christmas party at the Swan pub at Stockwell. He would like to invite you.'

'When is the party?'

'It's on Friday.'

'Sorry,' I said, 'I'm busy.'

For the second time I left the room and went upstairs to get my coat. Mike tidied up and followed me up the stairs.

'Mike Fisher is a very good instructing solicitor,' he said.

'Yes,' I said, 'and he's quite attractive.'

'He would like you to go to the party on Friday.'

'I'm busy. Sorry I can't make it.'

'I don't think you understand, Constance. He has asked if you will go and I have told him that you will be there.'

'Oh well, in that case Mike, I'll be going to the party on Friday!'

He laughed, and so did I. He knew very well that I did not have a choice in the matter – when your pupil master tells you to go, you go.

I turned up for the party on Friday and most of Chambers were there with the curious exception of Janet Plange, Christiana Hyde and Sandra Grayham. There were hundreds of people, most of whom I did not know. Mike Mansfield was there dancing away with anyone who wanted to dance with him. I decided he was bit of a flirt. Mike Fisher came over when I was on my own. He bought me a drink and then we had a dance, but not a close dance. He joked a lot. I liked him. We spent much of the evening talking to each other and at the end of the evening he offered me a lift home. It was on his way and he lived fairly close by. As he dropped me off he suggested that we meet up again soon. I agreed to that. Soon meant before Christmas. I agreed to that too.

There was much talk in Chambers the following day, mainly about me. The speculation was whether Mike Fisher and I were going to become an item. We were not, but it did not stop the gossip. I heard someone say 'She doesn't let the grass grow under her feet.' Fortunately Chambers closed soon for the Christmas break. On Christmas Eve I got a call from Mike Fisher. He wanted to know what I was doing. I was doing nothing much. I wanted some space to myself and that meant I would spend Christmas as I usually did – on my own. I told him I had already made my Christmas arrangements and he did not question me further. I agreed to see him after the break. Soon after Boxing Day I was invited round to his flat. It was very impressive, full of lots of modern art. I thought he had excellent taste. I decided we would become good friends. I would not let it develop into a significant romance and I sensed that he preferred it that way.

Early in the New Year I went back to Tooks Court. Mike Mansfield was due to start a murder case at the Old Bailey before going back to Sheffield for more cases concerning the miners. Spending more time in Tooks Court was painful. I got on well with the senior members, but all the pupils seemed to have a hard time from the three most junior tenants. I consoled myself that it was not only me. Whenever Mike was in Chambers, he was always offered one of Janet Plange's special biscuits and a nice cup of tea which she made herself. If I was present in the room at the time, I would be offered one. I would, of course, always refuse.

Working with Mike Mansfield was brilliant, his technique in court was really in your face, but at the same time subtle. He could tie a witness up in knots. They would leave the witness box covered in confusion and, I suspect, wondering how they got there the first place. Every pupil tends to hero-worship their pupil master, but mine really was a star. I sat behind him every day and looked forward to the forensic battle. Win or lose, Mike Mansfield was brilliant, and very few barristers were in his league.

It was after a triumphant day in court in late January that I was informed by Janet that there had been a meeting in Chambers concerning my fares to Sheffield. A sub-committee had been formed to determine my application for assistance. Before that could be done, the committee needed more information.

'Janet,' I said, 'I did not apply for assistance and I do not want it. I am not eligible. Would you please remove my name from your list.'

'I'm afraid you are eligible, Constance, because you are a pupil and we have been through this before. You cannot opt out.'

Janet handed me a list of questions that required answers. I filled it out and returned it to her.

'You should have a decision,' she said, 'by the end of next week.'

The wives of the miners were coming to London to take their cause to the streets. Chambers had put round a note saying that the ladies required accommodation and food for the time that they were in London. If anyone could put them up, even on the floor, we should put our names forward.

'Sorry, can't help out,' said Sandra.

Janet was reading the note again.

'I don't think I can help out. Constance, what about you? Can you offer accommodation? You put down on your fare application that you own a house.'

'I don't know, Janet, I might be able to.'

'Well, shall I just write here "possible accommodation"?'

'Yes, Janet, that is a good idea.'

'And how many?'

'Possibly three but I need to think about it.'

'And just where are you going to put them?'

'I don't know yet, on the floor I suppose.'

'Well maybe I need to reconsider,' said Janet.

'Not me,' said Sandra, 'I don't want them on my floor.'

It did not take me long to decide I would provide accommodation for three ladies in Clapham and I would assist them to collect funds. The ladies would arrive with their sleeping bags, slogans and collection boxes and I would go with them and encourage members of the public to part with their money, preferably into the collection boxes. Let's hope they were sympathetic to the miners' cause.

*   *   *

The ladies turned up on Friday, they were from a pit colliery in Orgreave and they had been badly affected. There was no money coming into the house. Their husbands were not entitled to any wages, because they were on strike, and the government were not going to provide assistance. There were still mouths to feed and so the ladies came to the streets of London. The other factor, I suppose, was that they wanted to feel part of the action.

During their time with me we went out collecting every day. We got up at six o'clock and had set up outside the allocated train station by seven or seven thirty. With our banners up and our collection boxes out, the ladies sang and preached the cause to those who passed by. I was quite content to shake my collection box at anyone who came close enough to put money in the box. It was hard work begging, standing there in the cold with just a flask of tea and a home made sandwich. The first day I had not put enough clothes on. My feet got cramp and by the end of the day I was frozen. The ladies were made of sterner stuff. I did not complain and I did not leave early. I stayed all day and at about eight pm we made our way back to my place.

The following day I was too warm – in extra pairs of leggings, jumpers and gloves. We collected rather a lot of money. The strike was not brought on by the women; they did not ask for it, but it was their children who were suffering. Children had a difficult enough time as it was. By the time the ladies were packing up to go I was exhausted. No more collections; that was a relief to me. I don't think I would want to do that every day. The ladies returned to Orgreave and I returned to my work.

We had one more week at the Old Bailey with Mike defending in a murder case where the defendant had allegedly murdered an acquaintance and then chopped him up with a sharp instrument and sold the body as meat in the local pub. He did not really have a defence as far as I was concerned, but Mike ran the 'not me' defence and challenged every aspect of the prosecution's case. It was a horrendous case. Mike's forensic skills were superb and I learned a great deal. The same evening I was having a cup of tea, at my desk, reading up on the next case when Janet Plange returned. Behind her was Sandra Grayham, who first went into her own room to drop off her bags then returned to ours.

'Hi,' I said, looking up briefly.

'Oh, Constance,' said Janet, 'leave us will you?'

'Sure,' I said and I went and sat at Christiana Hyde's desk, taking my bag with me. I had some research I could get on with until I had my desk back. Fifteen minutes later, Janet Plange shouted through.

'Constance, would you like to come in here please? Do take a seat. I've got a bit of bad news, I'm afraid.'

'What's that, Janet?'

'The application you put in for assistance with your fares has been means tested and it has been decided that you are not eligible.'

I wanted to laugh but restrained myself.

'We can give reasons if you wish, but you will have to put that request in writing.'

'Oh, no, that is not necessary. Thank you for telling me,' I said.

'Not a problem,' she said. 'You can go now.'

I was relieved. An application I had never wanted to make had been rejected. It was hilarious. I did not give tuppence for assistance with fares. I had been travelling up and down from Sheffield without anyone ever asking me how I managed and then I had to go through this farce only to be told that I could not get any assistance anyway. What a waste of time!

I had some photocopying to do. The copier was in the Clerk's room just in front of Paddy O'Connor's room, which looked out towards the back of the building. Paddy was a member of Chambers I'd immediately liked when I first met him. He was a perfectionist with a bit of a sniff now and then. He was very charming to me. He was married to one of the most attractive women at the Bar. He had very little time for those who were intellectually challenged. He was good looking, even with his specs on, and had a very nice voice, clear eyes and quite a fit physique. When I reached the photocopier, there was a new face copying some authorities.

'I don't believe we've met,' he said. 'I'm Adrian Fulford.'

'I'm Constance Briscoe.'

'If there is anything I can assist you with, do ask,' he said.

He was charming. I came to use his initials when referring to him, but for me A.F. meant absolutely fabulous. He was very attractive, but I decided he was a little too perfect to be my type and anyway he was too young. I did know that he would become a friend.

A little later that day Helena Kennedy popped in. She was a Glaswegian with quite a strong accent. I thought that I was short but she was even shorter than me. I had seen her before on telly and in the papers. I had even heard her on the radio. She was very passionate about equality, fairness and human rights. She was trying to find a babysitter, because she had been let down with her previous arrangements. I offered to do it. I was free and she lived in Tottenham Court Road, which was not that far away.

That Sunday I travelled to Sheffield. We were there for many weeks, travelling home at the weekends. Mike Mansfield was, as ever, brilliant. Tony Gifford, who was head of Wellington Street Chambers, was also in Sheffield. He was involved in another trial involving the miners. I met him at a social function. I knew he was a Lord, but he did not have any airs and graces, he was very down to earth. The first time I met him he said I should call him Tony. We got on very well. Tony came from the kind of privileged background that I could not even dream of, but yet he had a social conscience. Our lives linked momentarily through the miners' strike. I wondered if he would have had a social conscience if he had not had a privileged background. With my background, I had more in common with the miners than with the lawyers. We were born into circumstances beyond our control and, if given a choice, would probably have made a few changes.

12
A Brief's Life

1985

In April 1985 we were having another special session with Janet Plange and Sandra Grayham when Janet spoke.

'Now do tell me, Constance, can you please, where Edmonton County Court is?'

'I've got no idea,' I said.

'What about Horseferry Road Magistrates' Court?' said Sandra.

'Don't know,' I said, 'but it must be on Horseferry Road.'

'I see,' said Janet, 'and Wandsworth County Court?'

'I don't know.'

'Well, what about Camberwell Magistrate's Court?'

'Yes, I know where that is. I've been there.'

That was where I had summonsed my stepfather when he put my head through a window.

'What about Highbury Corner Magistrates' Court?'

'I don't know, I would have to look it up.'

'Well, Constance,' said Janet Plange, 'this is very serious.'

'What's serious?' I said, none the wiser.

'Constance,' she said, 'as a pupil you really must learn to speak when you are spoken to. It really does you no good at all to conduct yourself in this way, if you don't mind me saying so.'

I decided not to pursue it. If it was important it would come up again.

'Why do you wear make-up?' Sandra asked.

'It makes me feel better about myself.'

'Well,' said Sandra, 'you should try and do with less war paint.'

I had no intention of wearing less war paint, but I kept my counsel.

'Please excuse me,' I said. 'Thanks for your advice. I hope you don't mind, but I'm just going to pop next door and try and get some work done.' I picked up my stuff and disappeared. I had had enough of the pair of them and were it not for the fact that they would have a say about whether I was offered a permanent place in Chambers, I would have been less accommodating. I was now on a countdown to the end of my first six months' pupillage. During my second six I was entitled to be instructed by solicitors and appear in court to do my own applications, small uncomplicated summary trials and also to make appearances in the County Court. I was looking forward to this period – not only would I be in Court but I would get paid as well. Me, Constance Briscoe, counsel, getting paid to do what I had always wanted to do!

It was Helena Kennedy who first alerted me to the problems ahead. There had been a number of complaints about me raised by members of Chambers. Helena asked me to deal with them. Those who had complained were concerned that I lacked the experience to take my own cases. They were concerned on a number of fronts: the first was that I would embarrass the good name of Tooks Court, because I was softly spoken and would never make myself heard in court. I did not have the kind of voice that would carry. Cross examination would be a complete disaster. The second complaint was that I did not know my way around the Magistrates' Courts or even the County Courts and I seemed completely uninterested in familiarising myself with such courts. They said I had absolutely no experience of the lower courts, having spent all my time with Mike Mansfield. I would never do the type of work that he did and if I did it would not be for a very long time. For all these reasons I should not be let loose on the public, who were bound to suffer.

I was gobsmacked, speechless! It was obvious who had complained.

'Well, what do you say about this, Constance?'

'Well, it's certainly not true, Helena, and I know who's made those complaints,' I said.

'Go on, Constance, tell me, what do you say about these complaints?'

I sat with Helena and told her about life on the top floor, about the biscuits, the afternoon teas, the comments and atmosphere and the indignities that pupils have to suffer at the hands of the three most junior tenants at Tooks Court. Finally I told her about my experience. There could surely be no better education in advocacy that watching Mike Mansfield.

'I haven't been in the County Court, but I have seen loads of cases in the Magistrates' Court with Mike. I have a right to take cases in my own name and no one has yet said that I am incompetent.'

Helena asked me to leave it with her for the time being; she would take soundings and get back to me. About a week later, she informed me that she had called an extraordinary Chambers meeting, which I could attend in keeping with the policy of Chambers. She had spoken to Adrian Fulford who was very supportive. The meeting which was due to take place the following day would explore a number of issues including my second six months' pupillage. I asked whether I had to say anything, but Helena said that she would speak on my behalf. I had never imagined that I could be the centre of attention in this most unwelcome way, but I obviously couldn't accept the criticisms just like that. We had very little to say to each other on the top floor the afternoon before the Chambers meeting. I had no idea how tomorrow would end up, but I was not going to be defeated without a fight. I was happy for Helena to speak on my behalf, but if the time came when I thought she might need some additional help I would just speak out myself.

The following day I kept right out of the way, choosing to spend my time in the Inner Temple library. Just before five o'clock I made my way back to Tooks Court to meet my accusers face to face. I informed the clerks that I was back and made my way upstairs to wait until the appointed time. How some of them must have regretted the policy decision to allow pupils into a Chambers meeting! This was my first, and under Any Other Business was my name, Constance Briscoe.

We all gathered in the largest room in the building and the chairs were randomly placed. It was some time after five thirty when the meeting was quorate – inevitably it took time for people to return from court until the neccessary minimum were present. Sandra was there busying herself with absolutely nothing. Janet was there offering to make cups of tea. There were a lot of matters to be covered before they reached AOB. Various issues were discussed, from tenancy applications to the lack of space that the tenants had to work in.

After a little short of an hour and fifteen minutes my item was reached. Helena started. She spoke in a low but firm voice, her Scots accent giving her a business-like air. She said that there had been some criticisms of Constance Briscoe and, for those in the meeting who did not know Constance Briscoe, she was Mike Mansfield's pupil and was approaching the end of her first six. There had, however, been a number of complaints to the effect that she should not be starting her second six at the normal start date and instead it should be delayed to a non-specific date in the future. Since the consequences could be very serious for Constance, it was only fair that those who had these concerns should express them, so we could have a discussion about them.

I glanced over to Sandra Grayham, who was staring at her feet. Janet Plange was giving the impression that she was hearing these criticisms for the first time. As for Christiana

Hyde, she was distracted and looking the other way. As there was silence, Helena continued. She was determined that the matter should be dealt with properly. It had been said that Constance was softly spoken and would never be able to throw her voice in court and be an effective cross examiner. It had also been said that she did not know the difference between a Magistrates' Court and a County Court and furthermore would never even find her way to court. The meeting remained in oppressive silence. After a while, Helena spoke again. It had also been said that Constance would embarrass the good name of Tooks Court. These were very serious criticisms and it was only right in a fair minded Chambers like ours that Constance should know those who sought to criticise her. I waited with bated breath. There was utter silence, until Adrian Fulford started to speak.

'I support Helena. It would be monstrous for these Chambers to deny Constance the right to progress to the next stage without her having the opportunity to meet these criticisms head on.'

'Will anyone who has concerns speak now?' said Helena. It almost sounded like a marriage service.

There was an almighty silence. When it was obvious that no one was going to start the ball rolling, Helena began again:

'May I take it that there are no criticisms of Constance?'

Again, silence.

'This,' said Adrian, 'is your last opportunity to raise any concerns.'

Silence.

'Then,' said Helena, 'since there are no criticisms of Constance, may I therefore say on behalf of Chambers that we support her and welcome her and what Constance needs is encouragement, and given these Chambers I am confident that Constance will get the support she deserves.'

'Hear, hear,' said Adrian.

Sandra did not look up once, nor did Janet Plange. I had come through round one, but we all knew that the battle was far from over. It did not matter. I, Constance Briscoe, was ready to start my second six months' pupillage with the full backing of Chambers and no criticisms that any member dared to voice publicly.

13
Case Studies

1985

Some people obviously continued to voice concerns about me privately because after the meeting, when there were still a few weeks before I could stand on my own feet, it was decided that I would no longer go around with Mike. It would be a long time before I could do the kind of work that he did, so I had to get more experience of the sort of cases that I would eventually do myself. I was perfectly happy with that. I was told to follow Sandra Grayham to Court. I feared this. The idea of spending two weeks with someone I did not particularly get on with was alarming.

The following Monday, Sandra was due to start a trial at Camberwell Green Magistrates' court. It was an assault on a police officer. I had arranged to get to the court at one o'clock, check on the noticeboard in which court the case was to be heard and meet Sandra outside the courtroom. I got there very early and found that the case was in Court One. This was extraordinary! Court One was where many years ago I had gone to start proceedings against my stepfather. The notice board that I was now looking at was the very one that had informed me then to go to Court One.

I went across the road for a cup of tea, and Sandra arrived just as I finished. She seemed to be angry about something, and had a very ill-tempered conversation with the list officer before going to the cells to see the client. I followed her. By the time she had had a similar run-in with the officers on duty downstairs, we were very late and the client was hopping mad.

'Where the bleeding hell have you been?' he said. 'I'm on in a minute.' Sandra was in no mood to exchange pleasantries with him.

'I was here half an hour ago,' she said, 'and if that dog-faced bastard had let me in when I pressed the bell, I'd be out of here by now.'

'They are all the same, miss,' said the client. 'Give 'em a bleeding uniform and they want to boss you about. Think they rule the bleeding world.'

I got my notebook out and started to make some notes. The client looked at me suspiciously.

'And who is she when she is at home?'

'Oh her, she is no one. She is just learning the ropes. She is just here to watch.'

'My name is Constance Briscoe and I'm pleased to meet you,' I said, holding out my hand. He didn't take it.

'Well, I don't think I can say the same,' he said. 'I don't wish to be rude or nothing, but I'm well pissed off. I shouldn't be in here.' He turned to Sandra. 'Miss, you're my brief, when you going to get me bail?'

'Bail?' said Sandra. 'We are here for a trial aren't we? Isn't it assault police?'

'It was self-defence, miss. He attacked me. How was I to know he was a police officer. He certainly did not act like one on the night, I can tell you. Bleeding pig, that's what he was, a pig. I can tell you, miss, I got nothing against coppers, but that one, he needs to be bleeding locked up.'

'So it's a not guilty then, is it?' said Sandra.

'Yeah, miss, for definite, not guilty.'

'And what about giving evidence, how do you feel about that? It's down to you,' said Sandra.

'Yeah, I don't mind, miss. I'll go into the dock and tell the judge what's what, for sure.'

'Good,' said Sandra. 'I'm sure I don't need to tell you with your previous, but if you attack the police officer's credibility the prosecution are entitled to put evidence of your bad character before the court. You understand me?'

'I'm a bit confused, miss, what bad character are you on about?'

'Well, you have two previous convictions for assault police. If your defence is that the police officer attacked you and you had to defend yourself, the prosecution will be entitled to tell the court about your previous convictions.'

'I can't see what that's got to do with it, miss. That's in the past. Maybe that's why he picked on me.'

'Well let's see how we go. I'll just go and sign on and let the court know that we are here.'

When we left, the jailer secured the cell door and flapped down the observation box, which is located at eye level in the steel door. As I left I saw the client combing his hair, smartening himself up ready for his day in court. As the jailer let us out of the cell area, he turned and smiled at Sandra.

'Have a good day, miss.'

'Have a good day yourself,' she said as she stalked up the stairs.

Back in the court's main hall, lawyers and their clients were in little groups finalising instructions. Sandra put her bag down at the back of the court and took her place in the front row. As she spread her papers out, I slipped into the row behind her in order to take a note.

'Sandra,' I said, 'is there any chance of me reading the papers or just the statement from the police officer and your client's instructions?'

She leant back and handed me four sheets of paper as the court clerk came in. She was an efficient looking woman in her late twenties. She wore a black cardigan buttoned up to the neck and black spectacles, which made her look studious. The ring on her left hand announced she was a missus and not a miss. A middle-aged man slipped into the other end of the front row and leant across to Sandra. He must be the prosecutor. I couldn't hear what he said, but I saw her shake her head. Maybe he expected a guilty plea. The court clerk enquired if they were both ready and they nodded.

'All rise,' she said and the magistrate took his seat. I had half hoped it would be the same one who tried my case against my stepfather all those years before, but I did not recognise him. He was a tall bald man, who walked with a slight stoop. He gave a smile of recognition to the prosecutor. The first matter took no time at all and we were on. The defendant was brought up to the dock. The prosecutor opened with the facts. The police officer was called to an incident in Peckham and when he arrived he noticed that a male and a female were fighting under a lamp post in a well lit area. As he and his colleague approached the fighting couple, he identified himself and told them to stand still. They did not and had to be physically separated. The officer had removed the female some distance from the male and when he was trying to calm the situation down and take particulars from her, a male, who was the defendant, crept up behind him and jumped on his back, knocking his helmet to the floor. In turn he fell to the floor and suffered minor abrasions to his leg and hands. As the officer tried to get the defendant off his back, he was called a wanker and a blue tosser (at this point the magistrate smiled thinly). When the officer tried to arrest the defendant, he struggled and kicked the officer in the groin. This action momentarily incapacitated the officer (the magistrate smiled thinly again). Other officers who had attended the scene restrained the defendant. He was placed in handcuffs and taken to the police station. On the way to the police station the officer noted that he smelt of intoxicating liquor. His eyes were glazed and he was unsteady on his feet. The officer concluded that he was drunk.

As the first witness was being called to give evidence, I took a closer look at prosecuting counsel. He was a short man, whose suit hung baggily from his shoulders. His hairline had receded all the way back to the top of his head and he had a few spikes of hair that appeared to be isolated on the left side of his head. His bushy eyebrows met in the middle.

The first witness was the officer who had been assaulted. He read his evidence in a stilted manner from his notebook. His evidence exactly matched the account the prosecutor had given in opening. When cross-examined by Sandra, he was adamant that the defendant had assaulted him and not the other way round. He had produced his baton, but only after the defendant assaulted him. He had not used it. Sandra suggested that the lighting was bad and the defendant might not have known he was a police officer. He said the incident occurred under a street light and he was in uniform. Sandra suggested he was not acting in the execution of his duty, but exceeding it by assaulting the defendant, who was only defending himself.

'No,' came the officer's reply firmly. 'That is not true, madam. It was your client who assaulted me.'

Another officer was called, who repeated the same story from the same notebook, which he had read and signed as correct immediately after it was completed. Then the evidence of the doctor who had examined the officer and the defendant was read. The officer had bruising and a graze, consistent with his account. The defendant had no injuries. The prosecutor closed his case.

Sandra Grayham stood up and called her client, but he remained seated. She called him again, then he got up and walked to the witness box and took the oath to tell the truth, the whole truth and nothing but the truth. He said he had seen a man and woman fighting and tried to interpose himself between them, when a third man with a stick approached him and threatened to hit him. Not realising he was a police officer he had struck him to prevent the attack.

Prosecuting counsel got to his feet as though in slow motion and took out a large red and white polka dot handkerchief, with which he rubbed his glasses. First he cleaned the left lens and then the right and when they were clean he raised them above his head, looked through them and then puffed on the lenses and began again to clean his left lens as he squinted at the defendant. After he had repeated this for the third time the magistrate tapped his pen in his ear, twirled it and then said: 'We are ready when you are.'

'Sir, the defendant has attacked the credibility of the police officer, I apply to cross-examine him as to his character.'

'Granted,' said the magistrate.

'Does that oath mean anything to you?' the prosecutor asked the defendant.

'Yeah.'

'Told the truth?

'Yeah.'

'Not waiting for God to strike you down.'

'What you on about?'

'The truth, to which you appear to be a stranger.'

The defendant started to shift uneasily.

'I am telling the truth.'

'Nervous about anything?'

'Well it's just the occasion, sir.'

'And you have had many such an occasion, haven't you?'

'Don't know what you mean, sir.'

'Well, you must have been surprised when you were arrested for nothing?'

'I was, sir.'

'And you must have been completely taken aback when you were charged?'

'Well, come to think about it now, yes sir.'

'And you must have been equally astonished when both the officers made lying statements, implicating you in a crime which they knew you had not committed?'

'Sir, I could not have put it better myself.'

'And when they both came to court and gave evidence against you, did you conclude that this was all part of a lying conspiracy?'

'A conspiracy, sir?'

'Yes, a conspiracy to get you by hook or by crook.'

'Yeah, I suppose so.'

'Did you know either of the officers?'

'No sir, never met them before in my life.'

'Do you know of any grudge they may have against you?'

'No, sir. They might have found out about my form and decided to do me.'

'But we can rule out any personal grudge?'

'If you wish, sir.'

'It's not as I wish. It's as you wish. It is not the first time that police officers have told a pack of lies against you, is it?'

'I don't know what you mean.'

'Well, did you not have the misfortune to be charged with an assault on a police officer three years ago?'

'Yes, but I was innocent.'

'You were tried at this court. Did you give evidence on oath on that occasion?'

'Yes I did.'

'And when you gave evidence did you promise to tell the truth, the whole truth and nothing but the truth?'

'Yeah.'

'Well, you were convicted, so may we conclude that the officers were believed and you were not?'

'I told the truth.'

'That was not the only occasion you were disbelieved on oath, was it?'

'Again, sir, I'm lost.'

'Three years earlier you were charged with affray and assault on a police officer and you elected to be tried at the Crown Court?'

'Yes. Sir, that is correct.'

'And you gave evidence, this time before a jury?'

'Yes sir.'

'And you were disbelieved on oath?'

'Well, you can put it that way, sir.'

'I do. You have heard evidence read about the officer's injuries?'

'Yes sir.'

'And you know that the doctor who examined him said that it was consistent with the account that he gave that he had been assaulted?'

'Yes sir.'

'And you had no injuries?'

'The bruises only come up later.'

'Draw them to anyone's attention?'

'They weren't that serious.'

'Did you see anyone else assault the officer on the night in question?'

'No sir.'

'Or anyone on his back?'

'No sir.'

'You're the one who's telling a pack of lies. You assaulted the officer and caused those injuries.'

Sandra did her best in her final submission, but the result was a foregone conclusion. The magistrate found the defendant guilty and because of his bad character sentenced him to four months' imprisonment. When we got outside, I asked Sandra whether she had expected that verdict.

'Yes, of course,' she said. 'It's hard to get an acquittal in the Magistrates' Court.'

The following day we were due to attend Marlborough Street Magistrates' Court. This was a most beautiful court at the back of Liberty's store, just off Regent Street. Sandra had to mitigate for a lady who had been shoplifting in nearby Oxford Street. We arranged to meet at the court at a quarter past nine in the morning, to go through the papers and take further instructions from the client. I arrived a little before nine and got myself a tea quite close to the court and waited for Sandra to arrive. Of all the courts I eventually visited, Marlborough Street was the most beautiful. It had an elaborate Edwardian exterior. There were only two courts and there were no conference rooms or toilet. If you wanted to excuse yourself, you had to go across the road, buy a coffee or tea and then ask to use their facilities. From the front door of the court, you had a direct view into the building and its L-shaped interior hall. There was a row of benches along the wall directly opposite the courtrooms for counsel and clients to sit on.

It was to be a quick in and out job. The client had pleaded guilty at a previous hearing and the case was adjourned for a Social Enquiry Report about her by the probation service. The main thing from the client's point of view was that she should not go to prison. Her reluctance was demonstrated by her failure to turn up. At ten o'clock Sandra started to pace up and down the waiting hall. She walked the entire length of the room and, when she got to the end, she would stop suddenly and then look down to the front entrance in a sort of trance for a few seconds. Then she walked back the length of the hall and repeated the exercise. No other counsel walked the length of the hall. At five past ten I asked Sandra if I could look inside both courts. She stayed in her trance and did not answer, so I slipped into Court One.

It was extremely disappointing. I was expecting an Elizabethan Hall, I don't know why. Maybe because of the court's external presentation. But it was a typical municipal building room, quite ordinary, or perhaps even plain.

It was a slightly chilly morning, but that made no difference to the list officer, who was in a white shirt, sleeves rolled up to the elbow, dark trousers and carried a clipboard of the list of the day's cases. He went out into the hall and as nothing was happening I followed.

'Anyone for Court One waiting to register?' he called out.

Sandra moved forward and informed him that her client had not turned up. She gave her name and went back to pacing the hall. The hall had filled up and all the seats on the front facing wall were occupied, not just with people, but with bags reserving the sitting area for someone who wanted to guarantee a seat on return. Some of the defendants looked quite prosperous. In fact the majority of the ladies, who were obviously not lawyers, were immaculately turned out in the latest fashions. Curiously there were more ladies than men.

'This really is a lovely court,' I said to the list officer, 'and so convenient.'

'Beautiful location miss, beautiful. I've been here for quite some time and I love it. Because it's a small court, there is not much hassle. We can't take the most serious cases, because we don't have the security for them.'

'Most of the ladies seem very well dressed for criminals,' I said. He threw back his head and laughed.

'We get 'em all here – rich girls thieving because they are bored, trannies and fannies.'

'Trannies and fannies?' I queried.

'Fannies are the tarts, prostitutes. The posh ones are from Shepherds' Market. It's more shepherdesses these days.'

I looked round curiously. I had never seen a prostitute. I couldn't imagine selling my body for money, but I suppose barristers sell their minds.

'Wait a mo, look over there.' He nodded towards a very elegant lady in a mint green crushed suit. She had gorgeous legs. 'Now she is here at least once every two to three months.'

'What's she done?' I asked.

'She's a tranny.'

'And what's that?'

He roared with laughter again.

'She is a tranny, a transvestite. She's been whoring down Oxford Street.'

'Oh,' I said, a bit shocked. I could not believe she was really a man.

I was brought back to reality when I heard Sandra complaining, 'You're late.'

The client was anxiously going through security. She had managed to drop most of her personal items on the floor. She was being body checked. The security officer passed the detector wand up and down her body. She looked tired – too many late nights. She had a very good figure, quite slim but with tits to die for. Before you actually got to her tits, though, the tired eyes got to you first. Her black miniskirt was just a little too short to be decent at this time in the morning. She had obviously not dressed for court. As she was cleared, a younger woman in her late teens came through and joined her. They came up the hall to Sandra.

'I'm sorry,' she said, wiping a hand across her eyes and smudging her heavy mascara.

'You're an hour late.'

'Yes, I know. I am so sorry. I just could not get the right connections on the buses and in the end I had to get a taxi.'

'Well, you should have left earlier. This is a court and you cannot afford to be late.'

'I said I'm sorry, there is nothing else I can do.'

'Well,' said Sandra moving towards the benches, 'come and sit down here.'

Sandra sat on the bench and went through her papers. The client stood opposite her with the young girl at her side.

'Now what was it that you nicked? Oh yeah, clothes, silly girl.'

'Yeah, it was a bit silly.'

'A pair of trousers and a sweater from Top Shop. Was it worth it?'

'Well, I don't think it was.'

'Well, you know it wasn't, otherwise you would not be here.'

The defendant looked anxiously at the younger woman.

'You've got a bit of previous,' said Sandra. 'How old are you?'

'Thirty-six,' she said.

'Getting on a bit, but aren't we all? You've also got a conviction for being a common prostitute.'

The client blushed and looked over her shoulder at the young girl. I got the impression that the girl had not heard what Sandra had said.

'Soliciting,' said Sandra staring directly at her client. 'Is that right?'

The client brought her hand up to her mouth as though she did not want the young lady to hear.

'Yes,' she whispered.

'Well, are you still on the game?'

'No, I am not,' said the client firmly.

The young lady began to cry.

'What will happen to mum?' she asked.

'Don't know.'

The girl cried more openly.

'It will be fine, petal,' said her mother, squeezing her daughter's hand.

'Why don't you go outside and get some fresh air,' said Sandra addressing her remarks to both of them.

'We'll wait here, thank you,' said her client.

Sandra went to see where we were in the list and I followed. As we got inside the door the list officer indicated there were two more cases in front of us.

'Sandra,' I whispered. 'I'm confused. What has the defendant's past conviction for prostitution got to do with shoplifting?' Sandra looked at me as though I was stupid. 'It was a long time ago,' I went on. 'Is it really relevant when she has pleaded guilty to theft?'

Sandra ignored me. The case was soon called on. The client stepped into the dock and the daughter took her place behind in the public gallery. The prosecuting counsel opened the case and informed the magistrate that the defendant was seen to select two items from the clothes rail. She was acting suspiciously, looking around herself and, when she thought that she was not being observed, she removed the items from the hangers and placed them folded up between her legs. She attempted to walk out of the store and when she got to the door she looked around once more and exited, turning left. She was arrested a few yards from the entrance and returned to the shop. In an interview room at the back of the store she removed the items from between her legs and apologised. All goods were recovered.

'And what is known about the defendant?' said the magistrate.

'She has one previous conviction, which you can see on the antecedents. It does not appear relevant,' said prosecuting counsel.

'I agree,' said the magistrate.

'She is aged thirty-six, she has three children and she is unemployed.'

Sandra stood up and told the magistrate how sorry her client was and how this was the first time that she had ever done anything like this. It was a moment of madness which would embarrass her for the rest of her life. She was depressed by not having enough income to support her family. She now wanted to close this chapter of her life as soon as possible. Her eldest daughter was in court, providing support.

The magistrate glanced at the daughter approvingly and invited the defendant to stand up. He told her that shoplifting was a very serious offence, because it affected all of us. Ordinary shoppers ended up footing the bill. He sentenced her to probation for two years and ordered her to pay a fine of £100 and costs of £45. Finally he informed her that if she did not cooperate with probation and she was returned to court, he would send her to prison.

Leaving the dock, she walked outside court. Sandra and I caught up with her in the waiting hall.

'Just before you go,' said Sandra, 'I need to tell you that if you don't pay the fine, you can be brought back to court and you can end up in prison. Can you pay it?'

'No,' said the defendant.

'Well, how are you going to pay it?'

'I don't know,' she said, 'but I will find a way. Come on, babe, let's go,' said the client, holding her hand out to her daughter. They linked arms and walked out of the court building.

'Well, that's gratitude for you,' Sandra said.

We took the number 23 bus back to Chambers. I was not happy with the way things had gone. There was really no need at all to cause the humiliation that obviously had been caused. Back in Chambers Sandra came into my room with her brief for the following day.

'Can you prepare that for tomorrow and we will talk about it later.'

This defendant was charged with possession of cannabis, assault on police and dangerous driving. The trial was due to be heard in the Tottenham Magistrates' Court in the afternoon. The police officer had observed the defendant driving erratically through a red light. The officer pursued the defendant and indicated for him to stop and pull over. It was alleged that the defendant did not stop, but sped off reaching speeds in excess of fifty miles per hour. The officer gave chase as the defendant tried to make good his getaway. Not only did he cross a pedestrian crossing at speed, causing members of the public to take preventative action to avoid an accident, he collided with a bollard as he turned right. As the officer approached the defendant's car he observed the defendant and another man get out and run away. The other man escaped, but the officer pursued Sandra's client. As he ran, the officer observed him putting his hand in the area of his groin and then he made a throwing action. A short time after that he was brought to the ground and apprehended. He was handcuffed and taken back to the location where he had been seen to throw something away and the package was retrieved. The contents were subsequently analysed and found to be cannabis. It was at that point that a violent struggle ensued with the defendant head-butting the officer and spitting in his face.

The defendant's account was a complete denial of possession of the drugs and he insisted that it was the officer who had assaulted him. He accepted that he did drive at excessive speeds, but he said he had not realised that the police were behind him or that they wanted him to stop. It was a straight-forward conflict on the facts, the defendant running self defence.

I looked up the legal definition of assaulting a police officer in the execution of his duty, together with self defence and possession of drugs. And dangerous driving. Once that was done, I photocopied the recent cases in the *Current Law Review* and then looked at the various other arguments that were open to the defendant. Late in the afternoon I presented Sandra with my research together with how I might defend if I were counsel. Sandra appeared quite pleased although she did not go through my work with me. She was busy on something else. She said I should come and see her later, but when I did she was still not ready to take me through the case. I did go back to her shortly after 5.30, but she was about to go home and told me that she would take me through the case in the morning at court.

Stopping off at the corner shop, I made my way home. I took my coat off and made myself a cup of tea. Sitting in front of the telly I didn't hear the phone at first as it rang in the distance. It must have been ringing a long time when I got to it.

'Hello,' I said.

'Constance, it's Sandra.'

'Hello Sandra.'

'Constance I have left my *Archbold* in Chambers. Will you bring it with you when you come to Tottenham?'

There was a bit of a silence and then I said, 'Of course.' I did not sleep at all well and the following morning I was up by 6.45. I went on the train back to Chambers to pick up Sandra's book and then on to Tottenham Magistrates' Court. Waiting for Sandra outside court I did not feel at all well.

When she turned up she was her usual self, loud and aggressive. The defendant arrived about fifteen minutes after Sandra and he too was in an aggressive mood. Standing about five foot seven, he wore a bobble hat pulled down low on his head. His features were very black. When he walked it was as if he had a slow melody in his step, but at the same time a sort of bounce in his left foot. He kept his hands in the pockets of a leather jacket and his trousers were bright white. They looked new. After the introductions, Sandra asked him to confirm his instructions.

'Pigs,' he said. 'Every one of them due to dead. Them hassle me family night and day, day and night all for what? Nothing. Them due to dead.' The more he spoke the more irate he got and Sandra nodded along as she took notes. Towards the end of his explanation he was pointing his finger at Sandra, jabbing at her in order to make his point. He had a control problem.

'Miss,' he said, 'if me did assault a police man him would ah dead. Look at my hands.' He opened his hands and turned them over, palm up. Sizing up his hands he splayed them and then closed his hand into a fist and turned his hand over again, palm side down. 'Look at my fist.' We looked at his fist but I was none the wiser. 'Look at my fist. You ever see a fist like this? If I take this fist and lick a police man, then him have to dead. Me would ah never lick a police officer to play with him. You think me ah joke with pigs?'

Sandra stopped writing and asked if he was sure he wanted to give evidence.

'You think me scared of them? Ah dead them have fee dead. Them don't want assault. Them want me fee lick them then them will know that is an assault.' Sandra's client was back to hopping from one foot to the other as he jabbed out indiscriminately into thin air. When he gave evidence he did not tone down the manner of his presentation. He lashed out with his hand demonstrating karate chops as he slowly swooped down in the witness box and then rose again in a semi circular twist with arms out in attack mode. As he explained what the police did that night, he growled at Sandra as he explained his hatred for them.

'Every one of them sick me to the pit of my stomach.' He simulated a gobby spit to the floor of the witness box. As if that was not enough he looked straight into the magistrate's eyes and said, 'I could have killed him if I wanted to. Yeah man, I could have killed him with my bare hands.' He displayed his hands again for the benefit of the magistrate. Sandra invited him to put his hands away. He did, but demonstrated a karate kick that almost dismantled the witness box.

Prosecuting counsel stood, but did not ask questions straight away. He waited for the defendant to complete his karate moves and when the defendant was quite still in the witness box, counsel asked him if he was finished. The defendant said he was and counsel began his cross-examination. He only asked a few questions.

'Did you perform those moves on the night in question?'

'For real,' came back the reply.

'Were they in self defence?'

'Yeah man.'

'I suggest to you that they were not in self defence, you attacked the police officer because with hands like yours you could kill him if you wanted to.'

'No,' said the defendant, as prosecution counsel sat down. The magistrate convicted the defendant and ordered a psychiatric report because, as the magistrate said, something was not quite right. Outside court the defendant was well pleased with himself.

'I tell them, miss,' he said to Sandra. 'I tell him you drop kick him, yes, why not? If the magistrate want I'll drop kick him too.'

He did not seem bothered when Sandra explained to him the magistrate's concerns. As he left court he jumped up into the air and performed a flying kick for the last time.

'Yeah man,' he said as he left the court. Sandra had tried to do her best to keep her client under control and to keep his hatred of the police hidden from the magistrate. She had failed, but maybe she was seeking the impossible.

14
A Bit of a Domestic

1985

I had had enough of watching Sandra. There was no way that I wanted to become the barrister that she obviously was. Surely it was better to compromise and avoid conflict where possible? Going back to Chambers, I tried to keep my head down and when I got an opportunity to talk to Mike, I explained to him that I had seen enough and wished to shadow someone else. He pressed me as to why I wanted to move on and I came clean. I found Sandra's manner too aggressive.

Mike arranged for me to shadow one of the male barristers. This I did for two days, but the following week I was detailed to follow Janet Plange. We spent most of our time in the Edmonton County Court where Janet's clients on the whole were women. Some of them had met extreme violence at the hands of their partners. The type of hearings Janet did were *ex parte* non-molestations and sometimes ouster orders, where the woman was seeking to get her male partner excluded from the house or to prevent him from assaulting or harassing her.

I found these cases quite difficult. The first time we turned up at court for a non-molestation order on notice, I walked into court behind Janet and met a sea of hostility. The parties were literally at each other's throats. The hall felt intimidating in a way that the Magistrates' Court never was. When Janet called out the name of her client, a woman strutted over in high heeled, white shoes and a low cut top. She was young, no more than mid twenties, and she already had three children. Her face was hard. Written over her features was the message that life had not been easy. Her skirt reached her upper thigh a good few inches above her knee and the hem rested on an expanse of bare white flesh. Her bosom looked ample in the low cut bra. It must just be heaven to wear a low cut top and never have to worry about how you look. I could never even imagine wearing such a top because of the scars I had on my breasts from my mother's treatment of me.

'He's over there,' she said, as she jerked her thumb over her right shoulder in the direction of a group of blokes. 'And another thing, I want him out.' Janet was very good with her client. She was very patient, introducing herself and then me.

'Why don't we step over here,' she said, as she touched her client's elbow to attract her attention. 'Just come over here with me.' Janet began to walk away, but her client was having none of it. She glared over her shoulder at the man who I assumed was her former partner.

'Well, what you waiting for?' she said to Janet. 'Go and get him.'

Janet explained that it was not her job to get anyone and the whole point of the hearing today was an *inter partes* non-molestation order which meant that the judge would hear from her and from her former partner before he decided what to do.

'Look at the gob on that,' said the client, staring at a young woman who had joined the group of men. 'Bleeding slag.' Looking beyond Janet's client, I could see the newcomer, quite a pretty girl, blonde, small, with a very dazzling smile. She kissed the respondent on the cheek. 'She ain't coming into court, 'cos if she is I ain't going in – tart.' The last word was shouted loud enough for the newcomer to hear. She ignored it. Janet tried to divert the client's attention away from the group and get her to concentrate on her own application for a non-molestation order.

'Have there been any recent events?' said Janet.

'What, sorry?' she said distractedly.

'Has he assaulted you? Has he been to the house? What has happened since you made your statement?'

'She's laughing at me,' said Janet's client at the top of her voice. 'She is having a bleeding laugh. Well, I don't find it funny.'

Janet explained that when the case was called on the judge would be very unimpressed if both parties were clearly hostile towards each other and, whilst she was not asking for her to get on with him, it was most important to be seen to be civilised and well behaved. The client postured for a while, shifting from high heel to high heel with her hands just inside the waistband of her barely there skirt.

'He is taking the piss and I don't like it,' she said to no one in particular.

'Well, you will just have to try and ignore him' said Janet, 'Don't let him get to you. What about the children, does he have access?'

'Yeah and no.'

'What does that mean?'

'Yeah, he does have access.'

'Right, then, how is it going?' said Janet. 'The judge might ask.'

'It's not going very well because I stopped it.'

'And why did you do that? Was he violent or abusive to you?'

'No.'

'To the children?'

'No.'

'Well, why did you stop it?'

''Cos I asked him to return my fridge freezer, which he removed without my permission, and I want it back.'

For a moment Janet stood with her mouth open and head half cocked, looking at her client.

'Sorry,' she said, 'I don't get this.'

'Well,' said the client. 'I want it back.'

'And what has that to do with access to the children?' said Janet.

She hopped from one foot to the other. 'I've told him that when I get it back, he can see the kids and not before.'

I was astounded at her bargaining skills and also at Janet's patience. Janet looked from her client to her solicitor, who had joined us, and back again.

'Oh I see, so if you get the fridge freezer back you will allow access, is that right?'

'Yep, it is,' she said rather pleased with herself. She glared over to where her partner was standing with his lawyer and flicked her head back in defiance.

'Tosser,' she said loud enough for him to hear. 'Two bit ponce.'

He gave her the V sign, then another for good measure. Then he stared down at his groin, raised his fingers to his lips, kissed them, turned round and patted his backside. His male companions started to laugh as they too gave the V sign towards her. I counted four of them before Janet told everyone to ignore them.

'God, how childish can you get?' she said.

Her client was not listening at all. She was posturing on her high heels muttering that she had had enough and pointing out her former partner had humiliated her.

'That's it,' she said. 'He can keep his frigging fridge. He ain't coming anywhere near us.'

'That is unfortunate,' said Janet. 'I really do think that is a great pity. We were doing so well. I can't tell the judge that we will negotiate a fridge freezer for access – he will think I am completely mad.'

'Well, that ain't on anyway. It's off. That'll teach him. He ain't seeing the kids ever again.'

'I do think we ought to be sensible about this,' said Janet, 'otherwise the judge will impose what he thinks is reasonable.

So we might as well come up with our own proposal rather than have it forced upon us.'

'I ain't budging,' she said.

'It is not a question of budging. If the judge orders it then you will have no choice in the matter.'

Janet was tapped on the arm by counsel representing her client's former partner.

'May I have a word when you are ready? We are against each other.'

'Sure,' said Janet, 'can you just give me a moment?'

Counsel walked away back to her client.

'Well what's it to be?' said Janet. 'We're about to be called into court. You can agree access now or let the judge decide. I can't wait all day.'

'Once a fortnight,' said the client, grumpily, 'as long as I don't have to see his ugly mush and he can pick them up from me mother's.'

Janet did not wait for a retraction. She was off to negotiate. I followed her. The solicitor stayed with the client, I suspect to prevent the breakout of yet another County Court war. The counsel on the other side seemed pretty sensible. She started by saying that her client did not particularly want to see his children at his former partner's address and would much prefer to pick them up at the appointed time from his mother or his former mother in law. It seemed like a deal could be struck in no time at all. He was prepared to accept access once a fortnight. Janet informed her client that the deal had been achieved, that her former partner would agree to her proposed access arrangements.

'Well, I don't agree to it. I've changed my mind. He ain't having no access and that's final.'

Janet set about the client, as did the solicitor. Both tried to elicit reasons why she might have changed her mind, but both failed. She would not budge on access. Forty three minutes later the client was still sticking to her final offer, which was no access at all.

'What about the fridge freezer you mentioned earlier?' said Janet.

'You can forget about the fridge. I told you that's off.'

'Well,' said Janet, 'I have warned you, you know, what the judge will say.

'Let him do it.'

The usher called on the case and Janet, her opponent and both the former partners made their way to the court. I walked behind the client. As we got to the doors of the court, Janet's client shouted out in a loud voice. 'All right then, at me mother's.' No one paid any attention to her. I have to confess I was rather looking forward to the judge's response.

'I said, all right then, at me mother's,' she repeated.

Janet turned round, as if she had not heard her the first time.

'So you are consenting, are you?'

'Yes.'

'As agreed?'

'Yes.'

'Why now? What took you so long?'

'I had to think about it.'

'And you've thought about it now, have you?'

'Yes.'

'And you agree to what's proposed?'

'Yes.'

'Right then, let's tell the judge.'

In court the issues were dealt with by way of a consent order to which both parties agreed. The judge commended both parties on the manner in which they had selflessly set aside their differences for the sake of the children. If only all cases could be settled so amicably.

Outside court we returned to exactly the same spot we had been before. So did her former partner. As Janet's client looked over to him he rubbed his nose using the V sign either side of his nose. Janet's client made an 'O' with her thumb and finger and started shaking her wrist up and down in a floppy movement.

'Wanker!' she shouted. 'Wanker!'

Janet explained the order to her client and we left court and made our way to Chambers.

In our room I unpacked my bag. Janet did the same. I was glad that Janet and I had got on so well during the morning and I admired the way she had dealt with her difficult client. I was about ten minutes into my next piece of work when Janet said 'Milk, no sugar, Constance.'

'Sorry?' I half turned round to face her.

'Milk, no sugar.' she said.

I got up and went off to make her a cup of tea. I placed it on her desk. She looked at it.

'It's not white enough.' She did not look up.

Off I went to get the milk. I poured it into the cup.

'Say when,' I said.

'When,' said Janet. I returned the milk to the kitchen and resumed my work.

15
Greenham Women

1985

That was it. My first six months had come to an end and I was now entitled to take my own cases. Although Helena Kennedy had apparently silenced those who were critical of me, I was all too conscious of the fact that those same individuals would watch my progress and make a careful note of cock-ups that might occur along the way. They had been unsuccessful in preventing me continuing to the second stage of my training, but I was fairly certain that the problems would crop up again when I applied for a permanent tenancy. In the meantime I would just enjoy my second six months' pupillage.

I was handed my first very own brief. A firm known by the initials YPLA had instructed me to represent a Richard F. I was to apply for Legal Aid and then to seek a remand of the hearing to another date. There were only ten lines of instructions, but I was so nervous that I kept reading them again and again. The defendant had been charged. The solicitors required an ad-journment to take instructions. That sounded fairly simple, but I just had to be prepared. I was over the moon with having my first brief.

I got up very early the next day, which was a Tuesday, so that I got to the Willesden Magistrates' Court well on time. In fact, I was so early that I had an hour's wait before the court opened. Popping across the road, I got myself a cup of tea and then waited on the doorstep. As the doors opened, we all filed into court. I went to the enquiry office to pick up my legal aid form and then went off to find my client. Standing in the court hall I shouted his name from time to time. Shortly after ten past ten, he arrived. I introduced myself. We found a quiet corner and I helped him to fill out the various forms. I did not tell him this was my first case ever. The case was called on and I walked into court and sat in counsel's row in my own right. My client made his way into the dock and the court clerk then confirmed his name as Richard F. The prosecutor stood to his feet.

'May it please your worship, I appear on behalf of the Crown. The defendant is represented by Miss Briscoe and this is a first appearance.'

Indeed it was, I thought. I stood up.

'May it please you, sir. I have filled out the legal aid forms and submitted them. May I please have an adjournment so that we can consider mode of trial on the next occasion? We have not been supplied with any statements in this case, but we have been served with a charge sheet and a case summary.'

'How much time do you require Miss Briscoe?'

'Four weeks, please.'

'Is there any objection to that?' asked the magistrate.

'No,' said the prosecutor. 'The defendant has been on police bail in his own recognisance of £100. We are content with that.'

'Stand please,' said the magistrate.

The defendant rose to his feet.

'This case is adjourned to June 26. Bail as before.'

'Next case,' said the court usher.

I made my way out of counsel's row and out of court to find my client. He was waiting for me. I stressed to him the importance of keeping out of trouble in the meantime and that he should keep in touch with his solicitor. 'That's it,' I thought as I made my way back to Chambers. I had actually opened my mouth in court. I was now a barrister with experience. I was pleased with my day's work. Back in Chambers, I called the solicitors and informed them of the day's proceedings and the next date in court. Endorsing my brief with the orders of the court, I filled out my legal aid form and returned the brief to the clerks, so they could make a note in the diary of the next court hearing.

I was extremely pleased when I was instructed as a noting brief in a case at Orgreave from June 6–14. The solicitors were the well known and respected firm of Birnbergs and the fee was £50 a day. Orgreave was already a by-word at the Bar. This was the battle between the Government and the miners. The Miners' Union confrontation with the Government had turned into all out war. I was at the sharp end of political drama. I was again invited to stay with Mike McColgan, who had put me up when I'd been in Sheffield before. I listened spellbound. The two Mikes were discussing the case. They were my friends.

Whenever I went back to London, I was surprised at the envy and suspicion amongst the three most junior tenants. It was a frequent complaint that they were not being clerked properly or that they were not being put forward for the high profile cases like Orgreave that arrived in Chambers. I spent my time keeping my head down and not getting involved, since I was not a tenant. It was important that I knew my place. I did not want to fall out with anyone.

I began to be briefed by another firm called Seifert Sedley. They were big players in human rights work and sent a lot of work to Chambers. A lot of the senior barristers went on holiday in August and this gave me my opportunity. Seifert Sedley's first brief to me was to represent a lady called Lyn B on August 19 1985 in Devizes Magistrates' Court. Lyn B was a high profile campaigner among the so-called Greenham Common Women. They were a group committed to protesting against the siting of nuclear weapons on British soil. There was a large American Air Force nuclear base at Greenham Common in Wiltshire and this was the focus of the women's activity. I was excited, since I was sympathetic to the cause, but did not have the courage they had to sleep out in the open on a hard bed or no bed at all. I had done enough of that when I was younger. I really admired the women. Some of them slept at the gate entrance to the nuclear site and, when the opportunity arose, they would protest, by covering equipment with paint or by damaging the perimeter fence, or occasionally getting into the base and causing disruption.

Devizes Magistrates' Court was a long way away and I had to get up to travel there at the crack of dawn. When I got to the court, Lyn B was already there, surrounded by other Greenham Common women and general well-wishers. She was charged with criminal damage. She was such a colourful lady, full of enthusiasm and hope for the future and completely adamant that we, every single one of us, had a duty to do what we could to free our country of nuclear missiles. I introduced myself to Lyn and explained to her that the case would not be heard that day. She would simply be required to enter her plea of not guilty, the magistrate would set a date for the trial and then would be the time for her to produce her witnesses.

As I talked to the women surrounding me, I got the clear impression that they had more experience than I had of the courts. Some of them had already been tried by the lay magistrates who sat today and they doubted that they would try the case fairly. Two them said that when the chairman tried them before, they were given an awful time and had been convicted. One of them asked if it were possible to get him to stand down on the grounds of bias? I had never met the chairman and I had no idea whether he had demonstrated that he was biased, but anything was possible. I agreed to look into the matter and then advise in due course. Lyn was happy with that approach, as were the other women with her. We were called into court and Lyn made her way into the dock. She was cheered by the women who were there to support and encourage her.

The chairman had Superman glasses on, which made him look like an alien because he was bald apart from a four-inch strip of hair that had been arranged on the top of his head. He had clearly had some trouble with it because it was not combed in an orderly fashion, but looked as if he had rubbed his head or run his fingers through the remaining strands of hair. He looked as though he had received a dose of electricity, which made his hair stand on end. His dark grey suit, brilliant white shirt and burgundy tie seemed out of place under his untidy hair. The two ladies either side of him were bottle blondes with stiff Brillo pad hair. It stood up away from their heads, perfectly curled. It would take a very stiff gust of wind to dislodge that hair.

'You Lyn B?' asked the clerk.

'I am,' said Lyn in a well educated, middle class voice.

'Sit down,' said the clerk.

The proceedings were over in a trice. A trial date was fixed for October 2, the prosecution undertook to serve the papers within three weeks and Lyn was bailed.

'Will you be here in October?' Lyn asked when we got outside.

'I have no idea,' I said. 'It depends on whether the solicitors want me on the full trial. They might want someone more senior. Good luck anyway.'

'I'd like you to do it,' said Lyn.

I could not think why, because I had hardly said anything.

'You'd better tell Seiferts,' I said.

We shook hands and then I shook hands with the supporters. I made my way back to the train station. It took hours to get back. There was no direct train and I had to make a number of changes to get the connections back to London. Arriving back at my desk exhausted, I rang the solicitor to report the progress of the case. Gracia Stephenson was in charge and it was she who had instructed me. She was a trainee solicitor. She had a nice friendly voice and I knew instantly that we would get on. She suggested we meet for a drink and I told her I could do with one. We agreed to meet in the Printers' Devil in Fetter Lane at six o'clock. I'd hardly put the phone down when Sandra Grayham appeared from nowhere.

'Did I hear you arranging to go drinking with Gracia Stephenson?'

'We are meeting up, yes,' I said.

'For drinks?'

'Yes, I've just done a case for her and we are going to discuss it. Is that a problem?'

'Well, I don't suppose it is, but you do know that pupils are not supposed to fraternise with Chambers' solicitors.'

'I am not exactly fraternising, Sandra. She is instructing me.'

'Even worse,' she said.

'Well, what do you suggest, Sandra? Do you think I should cancel?'

'It's a matter for you,' said Sandra, 'but you know my view.'

Sandra disappeared and I decided to ignore her while I endorsed my brief with the events of the day. When I'd returned my brief to the clerk's room, I rang Mike Fisher and asked whether he thought it was out of order to go for a drink with my instructing solicitor. He said 'Absolutely not.' I decided it could not possibly do any harm and set off.

Gracia Stephenson was in her second year of training to be a solicitor and spent most of her time representing the Greenham Common women. She had work coming out of her ears, she said, which suited me because I needed very much to demonstrate to Chambers that I was capable of doing the work and bringing new work into Chambers. She said Lyn B had rung up to say the women liked me and she wanted me to do the trial brief. I said I hadn't much experience, but she said that did not matter. We agreed to meet again soon. The next day Gracia Stephenson sent me another brief, this time for Tracey B, who had already been convicted of criminal damage and I was instructed to mitigate on her behalf, which I did.

By the end of September I had been instructed in quite a few summary trials, pleas in mitigation in the Magistrates' Court, the Crown Court and a number of *ex parte* injunctions and contested access hearings in the County Court. Although I was nervous to start off with, I soon grew in confidence. I always mastered my brief and did not make any mistakes.

Gracia Stephenson turned out to be a wonderful source of work. The fact that Lyn B had asked for me to represent her in her forthcoming trial meant that other similar cases poured in. The women were not averse to appearances in Court, since it publicised their cause. The three most junior tenants were aware of the fact that I, together with other pupils, was getting work in my own name. Mike Mansfield's Chambers had been set up with certain principles such as treating everybody with fairness. Every member of Chambers aspired to such goals, but I got the impression some aspired more than others. Helena Kennedy had asked me on a number of occasions if I would babysit for her son, which I was more than happy to do. On the occasions she had asked me I was free and happy to help out. It did not occur to me that such a move might be seen as me smarming up to Helena. It was not an invitation limited to me – anyone could have said 'yes', but no one did. I began to realise, however, that this was not improving my relationship with the ladies on the top floor.

16
A Chick with No Dick

1986

I was feeling quite upbeat. It was now August and I had had some fantastic work and obtained some extremely good results. I was not in the slightest bit concerned when Tooks Court advertised for junior tenants to apply to join Chambers. The advert gave a deadline and all applications had to be accompanied by a curriculum vitae, references and reasons why the applicant wanted to join Chambers. Even though I was already known to Chambers, I thought I should approach the situation in the same way as an outside candidate. I set to work immediately. I consulted a number of solicitors who had instructed me over the past months and all of them said that they would be happy to provide a reference in writing and a copy to me. I then contacted Mike Mansfield and asked if we could meet up and he agreed. The arrangement was for the following week and we agreed it would take place at 6 pm. I was reading the advert again when Janet Plange came into the room.

'Are we advertising for tenants?' she said.

'Yes.'

'And just remind me, Constance, what is the closing date?'

'It is the end of August.'

I got my CV together over the following week and I had to ring a number of firms to remind them that I was waiting for a reference. Mike Fisher said he would support my application. I met with Mike Mansfield in his room and asked him about the advert for new junior tenants. What were my chances? Should I apply elsewhere and not bother with Tooks Court? Mike thought about it and told me that he would support my application to join Tooks Court. He had received very good feedback about me – my client handling was excellent and by all accounts I had a number of solicitors who spoke quite well of me.

'Do not apply to any other Chambers until a decision has been made here,' Mike emphasised, 'I can't guarantee a tenancy, but I do hope that Chambers will listen to me.'

That was good enough for me. Surely if Mike recommended me the Chambers would give me a tenancy?

'Mike,' I said, 'are there any issues that I need to address? Are there any areas that could be improved that you are aware of?'

Mike thought about it and started to laugh.

'No, Constance,' he said. 'I am not aware of any areas that you might wish to improve but tell me, how do you get on with the junior members of Chambers?'

It was my turn to laugh.

'I try my best, Mike, but it is not easy.'

'And what does that mean?'

'Mike, I do not want to say more about it than that.'

Mike caught my eye and I knew he understood.

The following two weeks I had a string of good results. On October 2 Lyn B was found not guilty of criminal damage. She had run the defence of lawful excuse and a complete denial of the alleged criminal damage. The magistrate heard the evidence and then ruled that the prosecution had not proved the case against Lyn B and he therefore found her not guilty. Her followers were ecstatic, kissing and hugging everyone in sight. On October 3, at Lambeth County Court, I successfully applied to have a respondent who had breached an order of the court committed to prison. The same day another client, Leslie C, narrowly escaped a prison sentence at Tonbridge Magistrates' Court. I had succeeded in two cases on one day.

I got my application for a tenancy in on time and for a

moment I allowed myself to believe that I had a fantastic chance of Tooks Court inviting me to become a member of Chambers. They did not really need references to tell them what I was about, they knew from what they had seen and heard of me themselves. I was secretly hoping that the in-house pupils would be considered first and a decision reached on them before external candidates were interviewed. My hopes of that were dashed when I received a letter signed by Mike Mansfield.

September 3, 1986

Dear Constance,

We have decided to consider your application for a tenancy during the month of October, when we will be considering all other such applications. We would like to point out that should your application fail, you will be expected to leave Tooks Court on or before 31st December 1986. No further extension of time will be granted after that date.

Yours sincerely

Michael Mansfield

This was not the news I wanted to hear. I rang Mike and arranged to go and talk to him.

'Mike,' I said, 'about this letter.' I put it on the desk and Mike read it.

'Yes, Constance? What do you want to know?'

'Well, firstly, how many people am I competing with?'

'We don't know until the closing date, Constance.'

'But I thought, Mike, that you would look at filling the vacancy from those pupils you had in Chambers.'

'Well, a decision was taken to advertise.'

'It says here that if I'm not successful I will have to leave Chambers by December 31, 1986.'

'Well, Constance, we can discuss that nearer the time, but don't worry about it at the moment.'

'If I am rejected, December 31 is simply not enough time to find somewhere else to go.'

'Well, Constance, why don't we just wait and see what happens? I can assure you that no one will throw you out if you can show that you have taken all steps to find somewhere else to go. I do think that you have very little to worry about.'

The following day I was instructed by Robert Brown of Darlington and Parkinson in a short remand hearing at Old Street Magistrates' Court for a trial. It was at the very least an opportunity to get yet another reference just in case I needed it. Over the next few weeks I tried to put out of my mind the inevitable short list and interview. I had no idea how we would be assessed or even what matters they would take into consideration. I kept my ear close to the ground and what I learnt was horrendous. In the first week forty applications came in and by the second week they were up to a hundred and three. The thought of all that competition made me giddy, but then again the positive way to look at the situation was to say that I had a more than equal chance.

At the closing date, I asked Mike how many applications there had been and he said a hundred and twenty-seven. I felt ill. In my worst nightmare I never expected so many people competing with me, no doubt many with much more experience. Looking back, I suppose the competition was stiff because Tooks Court was a division one set of Chambers, which everyone wanted to join. Because of the overwhelming response to the advert we were informed that Chambers would not consider my application in October. I asked when it would be considered, but Chambers were unable to say. It was only a week later that I was told it would be in November, which really was leaving things a bit tight if unsuccessful pupils were expected to leave in December. My head was in a whirl and so I decided to get more of my instructing solicitors to write references on my behalf, since they could provide information with regard to the cases that I had done.

Over the following weeks Mike was not around very much in Chambers and it was just not possible to get any information out of anyone else. The selection process started almost immediately and we were informed that the Selection Committee, which comprised mainly junior members supervised by two senior members of Chambers, would look through the applications to see who would go through to the next stage.

During this period I spent very little time in Chambers. I did not wish inadvertently to upset anyone. Nevertheless I did pick up a rumour that the first part of the interview process had concluded and that I had got through to the next stage. I am not sure how this information reached me, but I hoped that it was true. I kept the information to myself and waited for confirmation. It came the following Monday when Mike came in the room.

'I gather that you have got through to the next stage, Constance.'

'Yes, that's good, Mike,' I said, trying to sound as downbeat as possible. 'What happens next?'

'Well, everyone will be interviewed apart from our pupils because we know them already and after that we will decide, I think, but you will have to ask the Selection Committee. I am only the Head of Chambers. We do things democratically.'

I decided against asking the Selection Committee. It was now October and I was sure that we would hear soon. I checked my references to make sure that they were in order and that I had left nothing out.

So many had come in that I had a full file. The first was from Jane Wright of John Gittens & Co Solicitors.

Dear Mr Mansfield,
  Re Constance Briscoe
  I understand that Ms Briscoe is applying for a tenancy with your Chambers and that it was considered that it would be helpful for solicitors who had instructed Ms Briscoe to provide

a resumé of the work she has done for them. I have instructed Ms Briscoe solely in family matters, mainly in domestic violence and custody disputes. Some of these matters have required a considerable degree of competence and I have been surprised by Ms Briscoe's abilities, given that she is still only a pupil. I believe that custody disputes in particular require a great deal of tact and thoroughness and Ms Briscoe has shown herself able to use the qualities which she has to resolve different situations. I have found her work to be extremely thorough and she shows considerable understanding and sympathy with clients, who have told me that they wish me to instruct her again on their behalf. Miss Briscoe has shown that she is prepared to go to considerable lengths to assist the client, which I also believe is essential if counsel is to represent the client properly.

I would have no doubt about continuing to instruct Constance Briscoe. If you require further information from me please do not hesitate to contact me.

Your sincerely,

Jane Wright

John Gittens & Co

I have many such Dear Michael Mansfields from every imaginable source.

A few days later I was informed officially that I was in the next round, but it was with forty five others. The interviews would take place in the following week over a three-day period. Despite what I had been told earlier, I was asked to attend for an interview at 6.30 pm and was interviewed by a senior member of Chambers, a junior tenant and a middle ranker who was female. I entered the conference room and the Chambers' tenants introduced themselves to me and I nodded. The interview lasted twenty minutes and during that time I was asked a series of 'What would you do' questions, which really just required the application of common sense. I was told that we would all be informed within three days whether we had got through to the next stage. I appeared to have done all right. As I walked out of Chambers I felt relieved that it was all over for now. The whole process was nerve-wracking.

At court the next day I found appearances could be deceptive. I was representing a voluptuous young woman called Daisy. She had been strutting her stuff on the corner of Love Grove when the boys in blue crawled by. It was not like her to miss them. Normally she would have sniffed them out a mile off. She decided to brazen it out and slunk up to them like an alley cat.

'Want some fun, boys?'

'What do you have in mind?' said the driver.

'Whatever,' she replied.

'What do I get for twenty quid?' asked the one in the back.

'A full frontal and a double shine.'

'Get in,' said the driver.

Daisy got into the front seat beside him, pulled up her mini skirt and parted her legs.

'What's your name?'

'Is it relevant?'

'Yeah, I guess so.'

'Daisy, it's Daisy.'

'Well now, Daisy, what do you say if we go round the corner and you can turn your tricks?'

'Sounds good to me.'

Driving round the corner, he parked up and reclined the front seat. He paused for a moment.

'I would cover up if I were you.'

'Why's that?'

'Because you are under arrest. I am arresting you for being a common prostitute. You do not have to say anything, but anything that you do say will be taken down and may be given in evidence against you.

Back at the station, Daisy went mad. She kicked off so badly they called a police surgeon and it was then that her gender reassignment was discovered. The officer changed the charge to importuning for an immoral purpose *as a man*. Daisy was gutted. She pointed to her twenty-six previous convictions for common prostitution. They were her greatest achievement. Pleading with the custody sergeant that she hadn't had a dick for ten years got her nowhere.

The first thing she said to me when I met her at court was that she wanted the importuning charge dropped to a straightforward prostitution charge. She had come dressed to impress: red stilettoes, fur coat, diamante earrings, bright red lipstick and even a diamante tiara. Queen Daisy or nothing! The prosecutor's eyes opened wide open when he saw her, but he would not budge on the charge. In his book, even half a man counted as a man.

He opened the case to the jury, explaining that Daisy was born a man and his gender was defined at that stage. Though she had lived most of her adult life as a woman, that was irrelevant to the consideration of gender. On the night in question she was a man and was therefore importuning. Daisy's dignity was hurt. She felt called to act.

'Call me a man!' she shouted from the dock. 'Do I look like a man? Can you see a dick between my legs?'

The fur coat slipped from her shoulders and Daisy stood there stark naked. The jury started to giggle. The judge looked up and his jaw dropped. The dock officers tried to cover her up and failed.

'Well, hello boys. Here I am and I am all yours. Have you ever seen a finer pair of tits?'

'Put your coat on, madam,' said the judge, 'or I'll have you taken down.

Daisy just cupped her breasts, squeezed them together and blew him a kiss. That was the last we saw of her until lunch time. The judge called us to his room. The prosecutor wanted her charged with contempt, but the judge wanted to keep the trial on the road. He told us to be back at two o'clock.

Daisy was brought into the dock before the judge and jury and spotted the officer who had charged her. She turned towards him. Security had found her a skirt, but she lifted it.

'Call me a man! Have a look at my fanny. Take a long look. We have something in common. Neither of us have got any balls. That is why we get on so well.'

Security pulled her back. She re-arranged herself and smiled at the judge when he entered. She smiled at the jury when she gave her evidence. Some of them smiled back. This was the best show in town. They were only out ten minutes before returning a verdict of not guilty.

On November 18 I was overwhelmed to find that despite my worries, I was in the final three shortlisted candidates. I had heard that Chambers were hoping to take on between one and three pupils, which meant I stood a very good chance. Nevertheless I was careful not to appear smug or over confident so I could never be accused of arrogance. I simply got on with my work. I thought that the other two candidates were very good and, if they were offered a place, I would not have complained. We all knew that there was very little to choose between us. It took Chambers no time at all to decide on the remaining three. I was informed by a note that was on a Post-It note stuck to my pigeon hole in the clerks' room. It simply said:

November 26, 1985

Dear Constance,

Your application to join 14 Tooks Court has not been successful and you are now required to leave Chambers on or before December 31, 1986 in accordance with our letter to you of September 3, 1986.

It was unsigned. At first I thought it was a joke and I stood staring at the yellow Post-It, which had stuck to my hand. I looked up and around the clerks' room. It was so quiet that I realised they knew exactly what was unfolding. My head was in a whirl and I felt dizzy and sick. I was having trouble breathing and it felt as if I had just left the ground and was standing on thin air. I closed my eyes and counted to ten so that I could slow down the rush of blood to my head. The number thirty-five kept flashing up before my eyes and every time I blinked it disappeared, but suddenly appeared again and seemed to be approaching me at speed. There was another Post-It stuck to the pigeon hole of another pupil heaven knows what it said for I was beyond caring. I looked up and the senior clerk was sitting at his desk. I had always got on with him at a distance and he quite liked me.

'Are you . . . do you know which pupils were taken on?'

'Yes, miss.'

'Who?'

'None.'

'What do you mean, none?'

'That's what I said, miss.'

'So let me get this right, during the selection process a hundred and twenty-seven applied. We were short listed and short listed down to three and then Chambers decided to take no one on.'

'Yes, miss.'

Momentarily I did not know what to do, but then I thought, 'Well, there you go . . . all that drama and stress and after all these months 14 Tooks Court have decided to take not one single pupil on.' The reason to me was all too obvious. I concluded that the junior members of Chambers did not wish to take on anyone who might compete with them – what other reason could there be? The whole situation was ridiculous. I went off to find the other pupils in Chambers. None were in. It was much later when they came in that we all took in the true impact of what had taken place. We were all furious, but I could not see how our fury was going to help us. I had thirty-five days to get out of Chambers, to find another home. Christmas was approaching and Chambers would be reluctant to consider applications until after the vacation. I did not know what to do. My mouth was dry, my head hurt and I had a pain all the way down my spine. I sat at my desk and stared at my Post-It.

I was still at my desk praying for Mike to come in when, Janet turned up at about half past five.

'Hello, Constance,' she said cheerfully enough.

'Hello back,' I said as I continued my work.

She unpacked her bag facing the window, with her back to me.

'What sort of a day have you had, Constance?'

'A very good day, thank you,' I said. 'What sort of day have you had?'

'Oh, I'm exhausted,' she said.

At that moment Sandra Grayham appeared and was talking to Janet over my head. I continued with my work as Sandra glanced in my direction once.

'How was your day?' she said to Janet, as she perched on my desk.

'Oh, I'm exhausted,' said Janet Plange, 'exhausted and thirsty. How about a cup of tea?'

'Count me in,' said Sandra. 'Yes please. I never say no to a cup of tea.'

'Constance, are you all right?' said Janet.

'I am fine, Janet, thank you very much.' I did not look up.

'Two teas it is then,' said Sandra as she moved away and out of the door.

'Oh, don't you go,' said Janet Plange. 'I'm sure that Constance won't mind, will you, Constance?'

There was a hush while they waited for me to respond.

'Well, I'm rather busy at the moment, but if you are making a cup of tea I would not say no.'

There was a silence that went on forever and then both the

women just carried on as though I had not said a word. Whilst they were discussing the cases that each of them had been involved in during the day, I simply got on with my work as if nothing untoward had happened. From time to time I felt a glance come in my direction. It was half an hour later that Sandra left the room. Neither of them had gone to make a cup of tea.

'Are you sure you're all right?' I heard Janet say.

'Yes, why?' I said.

'Because you are not your usual self.'

'And what is my usual self?' I enquired.

She thought about it for a moment and did not answer. This was for the best, because I really was not feeling my usual self and knew that I might say something that I would regret. I was so upset with the ladies that I could barely speak. We worked in silence until Mike turned up late in the afternoon. He seemed in an upbeat mood and came in smiling..

'How are you, Constance?' said Mike.

'I'm not good, to tell you the truth, Mike.'

'Oh, Constance, well, is it something that I can help with?'

'I've no idea, Mike, but can I have a private word?'

'Do you want me to go?' said Janet.

'Yes,' I said, 'that might be a good idea, if you don't mind.'

Janet got up and packed her things as though it was a massive inconvenience.

'Mike, I'm told that you decided that no one should be taken on.' He looked mildly embarrassed, but waited for me to finish. 'I don't understand, Mike. Tooks Court went to all the trouble to advertise vacancies and then shortlisted the candidates down to three and then took no one on. It just seems a bit off to me – why go to all of that trouble if you were not going to take anyone on in the first place?'

'I don't think we knew at the time that we would not take anyone on.'

'Well, that's what happened and I would like to know why

no one was taken on and I am particularly interested to know why I was not taken on.'

Mike twirled his pen and raised his eyebrow as he considered what I had said.

'There were some very good candidates,' he said.

'Yes, I know that, Mike. I seem to remember that I was one of them, otherwise I would not have been shortlisted.'

'Well, that is one way of looking at it.'

'Is there another way, Mike?'

'I suppose not, Constance.'

'Well, why did Chambers decide that they would take on no one?'

'Well, I don't think I can answer that, but the problem was not one of ability, but balance.'

'And what does that mean, Mike?'

'It means, Constance, that there were concerns that we were a newish set where it is important for the junior end to develop properly. Some members of Chambers were concerned that, if we took on too many young barristers at the bottom end, it might cause problems for those members of Chambers who are trying to find their feet and establish themselves. I have to say I do not share that view.'

'So essentially, Mike – just tell me if I have got this wrong – the real problem is that the three most junior of Chambers don't want any competition.'

'That puts it rather bluntly. It was felt that there should be a limit on the numbers at any one level. As I say, it's a question of balance.'

'So where do I go from here, Mike? You told me not to apply to any other set of Chambers until these Chambers had decided and now I'll have to explain why my own set of Chambers has decided not to take me on after more than a year of pupillage.'

'Well,' said Mike, 'I am more than happy to help and will do all I can to make sure you are placed elsewhere.'

The conversation continued without a great deal of progress

being made. I did not ask whether Chambers would reconsider. in my view it was too late for that and it was clear to me that I would get nowhere with that request apart from further humiliation.

Mike made his excuses and left. He had yet another meeting to attend. I wondered if he would have the time to help me. Sandra and Janet came back. Soon their favourite topic came up.

'Would you like a cuppa?' said Janet to Sandra.

'Don't mind if I do.'

'Constance, would you like to make Sandra a cup of tea and I will have one too, thank you.'

'I'm very sorry,' I said, 'but I am busy at the moment. If you don't mind waiting, I'll do it when I have finished this piece of work.'

Janet Plange did not ask again. She could not really be seen too obviously be pulling rank over a pupil. She would never wish to be accused of that in Tooks Court, where pupils were treated as equals as a matter of policy. There was stunned silence for a few moments, as I rummaged around in my pencil case for a pen. The silence was broken by Janet uttering the words, 'I'll do it myself,' as she stamped out of the room. Sandra remained there for a few seconds more, but then left without saying a word.

I had really burnt my boats now, they would never forgive me for my impertinence in behaving like a tenant when I was in fact a pupil who had been given her marching orders.

I picked up all my belongings, tidied the desk and made my way downstairs. I had had enough and it was about time I went home. Stopping in at the clerks' room, I found there was more work for me the following day. At least my work had not dried up.

Out in the cool air I was furious. How could they refuse to take anyone on just because of a problem of balance at the junior end? That did not make sense at all. Tooks Court was not any old set of Chambers; it was supposed to give opportunity to those who were able to make a go of the Bar. The more I thought about it the more I thought that the whole system was unfair and needed to be challenged. At the very least I wanted an explanation.

I decided to write to every single member of Chambers and ask the reasons for my rejection. With twenty two days to go before I was effectively thrown out of Chambers, I drafted my letter.

> 14 Tooks Court
> Cursitor Street
> London EC4
> December 9, 1986

Dear Tooks Court members,

On the November 26 you made a decision not to invite me to be a member of your Chambers. I have seen all the references that were provided to you about my work. No one has suggested that there is any criticism either of my ability and potential as a barrister, or of my commitment to the goals which we share. In fact no reasons for your decision have been given to me at all. If you were an ordinary set of Chambers, I would have found it normal to be rejected on unspoken and irrational grounds, and I would have promptly set about finding a place elsewhere. However, you are a set which was established to further the struggle of oppressed people and to do so in a principled way. I believe in the goals of Tooks Court and I am sure you will agree it is reasonable to ask for your reasons for my rejection, in order that I may be better informed and to assist me in considering my future position.

Yours sincerely,
Constance Briscoe

I sealed each letter in an envelope marked PRIVATE AND CONFIDENTIAL with the name of the member of Chambers in large upper case bold font on the front. Shortly after eleven that night I returned to Chambers, letting myself in with my keys. The whole building was in darkness save for one room at the very top of the building. I made my way to the clerks' room. Switching on the light, I counted the number of pigeon holes. I had enough letters for each member of Chambers and I posted one in each pigeon hole. When I had finished I had quite a few spare envelopes so I stuck a letter in the pupils' pigeon hole. The clerks did not have a pigeon hole, so I placed one letter on the seat where the senior clerk sat and one for the second in charge. I still had spares so I posted the senior members again just to make sure that there could never be the suggestion that my letter somehow got lost in the post. Once I was satisfied that everyone had a copy of my letter, including Sandra Grayham, Christiana Hyde and Janet Plange, I switched off the lights, made my way back downstairs, double locked the door and went home.

I, of course, had thought about my actions and the consequences to me. It was possible that Mike Mansfield and other senior members of Chambers would take the view that I was just an uppity pupil out to cause trouble, but somehow I doubted that. In many ways I had been an ideal pupil: I had done as I was asked. I had made myself available at any time the tenants of Tooks Court required assistance. I had been treated by some members of Chambers like a modern day servant and still I had no complaint. It was doubtful whether the senior members of Chambers knew how those three junior members of Chambers behaved. I was quite convinced that if Chambers really knew they would have done something about it.

On Monday I was representing Neil M at Willesden Magistrates' Court. I had been instructed by the Young Persons Law Centre and my client had been accused of assaulting a police officer in the execution of his duty, and shoplifting. I had had a number of good results at the court and the stipendiary magistrate was known for his fairness and impartiality, although he did like to get on with the trial and did not like counsel cross examining forever when the clock was ticking away. I lost this time. At the end of the case I decided not to return to Chambers, but to go home and then phone in. I could always collect any work for the following day later. When I finally rang in, the Senior Clerk was in good spirits.

'Constance Briscoe,' he said, 'are you coming in?'

'No,' I said, 'unless you have work for me.'

'Well,' he said, 'just hold on one moment and I will check the diary.'

A few seconds later he returned to the phone.

'Yes, you are in court. The brief is in your pigeon hole.'

'I'll pick it up later,' I said.

'We look forward to seeing you,' he said, which caused me to panic. What did that mean, we look forward to seeing you? Did it have something to do with my letter? By now the whole of Chambers would have read their letters. Some of them, I was sure, would have been in a right flap: Helena Kennedy, for one and what about Mike Mansfield, poor old Mike Mansfield. How would he, my hero from way back, have received my letter? Would he think I should have accepted his offer of help and gone quietly? I imagined Sandra, Janet and Christiana scandalised over their tea and biscuits.

'Who does she think she is? Well, that's what you get when you don't interview for pupillage.'

On December 10 I went to Bow Street Magistrates' Court. It was quite an interesting case. The complainant had flagged down a police car in the middle of the night. When he approached the car it was obvious to the police that the man was in some distress. He had informed the police that he had been approached by a lady who told him that she had just been assaulted. He invited her to get into the back of his car with the intention of taking her to the nearest police station but as soon as she entered the car her distress disappeared and she started to rummage around in his jacket, which was neatly folded on the back seat. Although he told her not to, she continued. He stopped and approached the rear of the car, where there was a commotion in which he was assaulted. He managed to retrieve his wallet but she had made good her escape with twenty pounds that belonged to him.

Although this story might have sounded a bit dodgy, the incident had not occurred in an obvious red light district. The police radioed back to base and when the victim was in the back of the car the police drove around the area in the hope of apprehending the lady in question. After driving around for ten minutes the victim had shouted, 'There she is!' And there she was, in a high skirt and low blouse and red stiletto heels. The police approached her and informed her that an allegation had been made of robbery and the victim had identified her as the robber.

'He is a fucking liar,' she said as she tried to get at the back of the police car where she had rightly assumed the victim was sheltering. The police officer had removed her from the scene and cautioned her, which did not calm her down at all.

'He is a wanker, and if he ain't, then I must be Marilyn Monroe.'

The officer had reminded her that she need not say anything but that if she chose to do so he would make a note of what she said.

'Take a note,' she said 'make sure you get it down good and proper. You ready? Now that ponce that said I robbed him is a liar. He wanted a blow job doing and I charged him twenty pounds. We agreed the price and I got into the back of his car. When I finished he complained and said that he was not satisfied. He refused to pay me so I saw his wallet on the back seat and took twenty quid. Not a penny more not a penny less, just what we had agreed. He tried to stop me and he assaulted me. He put his hand up my skirt. I hit him and I want him done for indecent assault.'

The officer was quiet for a moment while he made a note of

what she had said and when he was satisfied that the note was accurate he invited her to sign it, which she did.

'Well' said the officer, 'if you have performed a blow job on him you should know the colour of his underpants. What colour are they?'

'Pink and orange spots.'

The officer made another note and again got her to sign it. The defendant remained with the accompanying officer as the first officer walked back to the patrol car. Relaying the conversation back to the senior officer the victim was invited to step out of the car.

'Would you mind dropping your trousers, sir.'

'For what reason, officer?'

'All will be explained, sir, but for the moment will you please just drop your trousers?'

Reluctantly he did and there they were for all to see: pink and orange spots.

'The lady claims to have performed a blow job on you, sir, and she correctly described the colour of your underwear. Do you know of any reason why she would know the colour of your underwear?'

The complainant could not give an answer at first and then said maybe they showed over the top of the waistband of his trousers. He still insisted that he had been assaulted and robbed and the defendant was charged. At the trial the complainant could give no better explanation as to how the defendant knew the colour of his underwear. The fact that the defendant had twenty-three previous convictions for being a common prostitute helped to persuade the court that the defendant had given a truthful account and she was found not guilty. All because of a doggy pair of underpants!

After that I rang Chambers to enquire whether there were any messages or work for me for the following day. The senior clerk said there was no work, but Mr Mansfield would like a word.

'I'll try and get hold of him later,' I said. 'It's not urgent, is it?'
'You tell me, Constance,' came back the reply. 'You tell me.'
'Well, I don't think it is. I think it can wait.'
I felt better when I got home.

Sooner or later I had to get on with applying to other sets of Chambers. It was now December 11 and in theory I had twenty days to go before Chambers required me to leave. Actually that was a complete fiction, because everybody knew that the last court day was Monday December 23 which was only twelve days away. That was the day when the Crown Courts closed down for the Christmas break and they would not re-open until Thursday January 2, by which time I would no longer be a member of Tooks Court. I did not go into Chambers the next day, but rang in at five o'clock to see if there was a brief for the following day. I spoke to Gavin the junior clerk.

'Constance, you are in court tomorrow. Your brief is in your pigeon hole.'

'Thanks Gavin,' I said. 'I'll pick it up later. Are there any messages?' Gavin checked the message book.

'Mr Mansfield would like a word.'

'Of course,' I said. 'Have you a number where I can get him?'

'No,' said Gavin. 'Mike does not give out his number, but I'll tell him to call you at home, if you like. When are you going to be in Chambers next?'

'Possibly tomorrow.'

'I think that Miss Kennedy was looking for you earlier as well,' said Gavin. 'I'll tell her you're at home.'

'Sure, Gavin, you do that.'

I stayed in until about half past nine, but didn't get a call from any member of Chambers so I set off to Tooks Court to pick up my brief. On arrival one or two people were about, but I was in and out so fast that there was simply no opportunity to stop and talk, much to my relief! I was beginning to regret writing all those letters.

My brief on Thursday December 12 was a bail application and then I had to mitigate a case that would be a plea. Gracia had asked for me: it was a domestic. It was my view that Dean B made my skin crawl. He was a nasty piece of work and I did not care tuppence for him, but I had to put my own views to one side. He was in the cells and feeling sorry for himself.

The police had gone round to his home address in response to an abandoned 999 call. There were sounds of a disturbance in the background. On arrival the police were met by Dean, who had some bruising to his face. He was asked to remain outside while an officer spoke to the occupant of the flat. She was Kirsty, a young woman in her twenties, who was Dean's ex-partner. They had been apart five years. Dean had an order banning him from coming to the house, but had come round anyway. They had had some verbal and in the middle of it he slapped her. She hit him back and then he broke her nose with an ashtray. She had needed twelve stitches to put her nose back together again. Dean was arrested and charged with causing actual bodily harm. The next morning he was bailed.

Some months later, Kirsty went with her two children, Aladdin and Charley, to the Charrington Bowl in Surrey. Despite the name, Aladdin was a girl. It had been arranged that they would meet their dad for an access visit. He offered to buy her a drink 'for old times' sake'. She agreed, but when he had bought her a drink he asked her who she was seeing. When she told him to mind his own business he got annoyed and poured his drink over her head. She gathered up the children and left. Dean caught up with her in the Tolworth underpass. He punched her head from behind.

'You bloody slut,' he shouted as the children began to cry. 'How many men have you been with? Go on, tell me Aladdin, Charley, how many men has your mother fucked when I'm paying her a one-er every week.'

A few more blows to the head and Kirsty was on the floor. As she shouted and screamed, Dean B stood over her with one hand on the wall to steady himself. He repeatedly kicked her in the head and ribs. Then he stamped on her head again and again. The airborne blood landed on the walls. Suddenly he noticed that Aladdin's shoe had come off as she ran for cover.

'Oh darling, you've only got one shoe on.'

As he put his daughter's shoe back on with his blood stained hands, he told Kirsty to get up. Crawling up the wall she left a blood smear trail behind her. When he was standing up B looked at her. She only had one eye open.

'If you ever stop me from seeing my kids, I'll send someone round to kill you. Now let's go home and have a nice cuppa tea.'

He grabbed her hand and started to walk off. Unfortunately for him, a bystander had already called the police.

'There's a man whose got a woman pinned to the floor and he's kicking her head in. He's in the underpass at Tolworth.'

There was a police car on the Tolworth roundabout. They stopped Dean as he came out of the underpass. Kirsty was caked in blood. Dean said it was 'just a little domestic'. An ambulance was called for her. Her face was an absolute mess. Dean was arrested and cautioned. He said that she had been asking for it. In the police car he confided in one of the officers.

'Just between you and me, off the record like, if you had two kids with a woman that you did not love what would you do about it? She gets everything from me. I pay her a one-er a week to keep the kids and she don't even teach them to read. They don't even know their alphabet. She's got blokes in and out of her house all day. She is just a slag.'

Kirsty arrived at the hospital and was seen by a senior house officer. He noted that she had extensive bruising around the left eye, tenderness over the left cheekbone and orbit and a fractured nose. There was a gaping three-centimetre laceration of the left ear and part of the earlobe was missing. She had a four centimetre laceration to the right scalp and her left eye was bleeding. She was admitted under a general anaesthetic to repair the ear and scalp laceration. After the operation she had to wear a head bandage for three days. Her stitches were removed seven days later. A month after that her laceration had healed well but she still had some blood in the left eye. The photographs taken before she was cleaned up clearly showed a foot print in blood across her face. On forensic examination it matched Dean's trainers. He was charged with causing grievous bodily harm with intent to do so.

He told me he had lived in hope that his ex would not attend the trial, but when he discovered that she and the bystander were at court ready to give evidence, he hit the wall again. He knew his case was hopeless. He had no defence. He had no choice but to plead guilty. He promised to get even with her when he got out. I mitigated for him that he had only acted as he did out of a desire to protect his children, witness that he had stopped to do up Aladdin's shoe. It had no effect.

'You,' said the judge, 'are a danger to women, especially those who have the misfortune to know you on more intimate terms. If you don't learn to control your temper, one day you will kill someone. You will go to prison for two and a half years.'

At the conclusion of the case I rang Chambers. Another junior clerk called Areyah answered.

'Constance, Mike Mansfield would like a word with you. He's been trying to get you now for a few days. Mike has suggested Friday 13 at six o'clock.'

'That's fine,' I said, 'I shall be there.'

Once the call was over I had a touch of the giddies. Friday 13 was not a propitious date.

My brief for the Friday was a straightforward plea in mitigation at Snaresbrook Crown Court. At the end of the hearing I packed my wig and gown and made my way back to Chambers. I endorsed my brief and returned to the clerks' room.

'Have you seen Mike?' I said.

'No,' one of the clerks shouted back, 'but he is looking for you and he is around.'

I went upstairs looking for Mike, he was not in his room or in Sandra's. If he wanted me, he would know that I was in my usual place. I had not yet been told whether I had any work for Monday and I had assumed that I was to be given my marching orders rather than wait until December 31.

Len Woodley passed by the door. He was quite a senior junior tenant. I had not had many dealings with him, but had always found him friendly and sympathetic. He doubled back into my room.

'Constance,' he said, 'I got your letter. Well, I think everyone got your letter. You've certainly put the cat amongst the pigeons. What I want to know is what reason they will give you.' He disappeared downstairs before I could respond.

Mike turned up shortly after six o'clock.

'Hello Constance. Thank you for coming and thank you for your letter, I'm very sorry that I have not got back to you before now, but I gather that we have been missing each other.'

'Yes, I think that is right.'

'And I needed to get a consensus from Chambers in order to answer your letter, which I am afraid I have not yet done. You know what it is like getting all the members of Chambers in the same place at the same time.'

'Yes, Mike, it can be difficult.'

'Anyway I have not been able to raise the matter with everyone in Chambers, but I thought you ought to know that we are dealing with your letter.'

'Yes, Mike.'

'The other thing is that I know that you are anxious about the deadline which is fast approaching. Chambers have decided that you should not feel under any pressure to go by the end of the month and, since you have raised an important issue in your letter, we are content to allow you to remain until we have responded to your letter.'

'Does that mean, Mike, that I can ignore that letter?'

'Yes, it does.'

'And does that mean that I will not be thrown out of Chambers?'

'Well, no one is going to throw you out of Chambers, Constance, but yes, you can remain here for the time being. I should also tell you that there will be an extraordinary Chambers meeting which will take place in the New Year. It is not feasible to deal with it before the break with Christmas fast approaching, and hopefully we will have some answers for you.'

'What, Mike, you mean you don't have answers for me now?'

'I did not say that, Constance. I said you will be provided with answers. How is work?'

'Couldn't be better.'

'And what about Chambers?'

'I get on with everyone as best I can, Mike, you know me.'

'Well, perhaps you ought to try a little harder.'

'And what does that mean, Mike?'

'It means that you should always continue to make an effort.'

'Well, I do, Mike.'

'In that case there is nothing to worry about.'

The meeting ended. I collected my work for the following week and left Chambers. Friday 13 had been lucky for me after all. I had been given a reprieve.

17
No Room at the Inn

I could not get out of bed on Saturday. I had a backache and a headache which caused me to stay in bed well into the afternoon. The stress was getting to me and it was making me ill. I had cramp in my legs and my arms ached. The truth was I did not want to stay at Tooks Court. I had had this fantasy, I suppose, this idea for so long in my head that I would be a tenant at Tooks Court. Mike rated me and he was so important in the scheme of things that surely I would be given tenancy. It simply did not occur to me that there would have been any problem along the way. Maybe I would have been better off in an old-style Chambers where the Head's word is law. I had not planned any escape route. I had no idea what to do apart from wait, see what Tooks Court had to say and in the meantime apply to other sets of Chambers in the hope that they would not hold the fact that Tooks Court had rejected me against me.

Some time after four o'clock I got up. Big Daddy, the wrestler, was on telly and he was fighting a mean fight. It was his wrestling techniques that had stood me in such good stead in my fights with my stepfather and at school. Big Daddy was declared the winner and the crowd roared. I felt better almost immediately. Big Daddy was a class act and wrestling was my favourite entertainment. If he could do it, so could I, even if it involved the odd foul along the way.

It was eleven days to Christmas and I had not received a single Christmas card. I had not even been shopping and I did not have a Christmas tree. If I was quick I could probably get one on the High Street, but I could not for the life of me think why I would wish to celebrate Christmas this year, when I had never really enjoyed Christmas in the past. I decided to go back to bed. I was feeling sorry for myself when I had no business to be. There were so many plusses in my life – it was better than it had ever been. I had a bed, food, clothes and a small but steady income. Constance Briscoe had arrived.

The following day my headache was as bad as ever and illness had taken over the rest of my body. I pulled the curtains around my four poster bed and curled up under my polyester duvet. My bed, which had given me so much pleasure and for which I had saved up forever, now imprisoned me. I could not turn to the left or right without causing myself serious discomfort. The pain was crawling down my spine and spreading out down my arms and legs. When I finally managed to turn from my side to my back, there in front of me was Miss K.

'What do you think you're doing, Clare?'

'Nothing, miss, I'm just not well at the moment.'

'Not well?' she said. 'You look perfectly all right to me.'

'I'm not well, miss.'

'How not well are you?'

'I'm just not well, miss.'

'Listen, Clare, if I can get up so can you. Not well is not having any legs. Now that's not well. A little bit of disappointment and you take to your bed. Get up, child, up up up.' Miss K was in her twinset – lime green jumper – and dog-tooth skirt. 'Get up, child, I'm going to leave for a moment and when I get back I want you up.'

Miss K disappeared and I started to cry. It was all I could do to turn my head. My neck was stiff with pain. Then Miss K was there on the side of the bed again.

'Well, child, are you going to move or do I have to make you?'

'It's OK, Miss K, I'm getting up.'

'And about time too. I'm surprised that you have time to feel sorry for yourself.'

'I don't feel sorry for myself.'

'Oh, child, don't be ridiculous. Now are you getting up or what?'

'I'm getting up.'

I must have dozed off, because I was woken up when someone slapped me across the face. There was no one in my room when I opened my eyes but my face was stinging. I dragged myself up and sat with some pillows behind my head. I had decided that I would go back to Tooks Court and, irrespective of my health, I would be at Barking Magistrates' Court next day representing two clients for Hodge Jones and Allen Solicitors.

I was glad Christmas was over. No Christmas presents, no cards, no telephone calls. It was not untypical of most of my Christmas celebrations. The period between Christmas and waiting to go back to work was worse than awful. There was nothing for me to do. The nursing agencies told me they were oversubscribed with staff. The hospice in Lyndhurst Gardens was cutting back on the use of auxiliary nurses in order to save money and they simply did not have any work for me. They did, however, let me know that if I ever wanted a permanent part time night auxiliary post I should not hesitate in letting them know.

Back at work on January 2, I was due to represent a client for new solicitors, Alex M, at Knightsbridge Crown Court. The trial was due to last several days, but, having had all vacation to prepare thoroughly, on my arrival the Crown made an application for an adjournment because they were not ready to proceed and much to my surprise the judge allowed the application. I was now out of work until January 7. I thanked the Lord next day when the same firm of solicitors came to my rescue. The defendant was due to appear at Acton Magistrates' Court for a simple remand hearing. I tried as much as possible to stay away from Chambers. I had developed the practice of going to court, doing my case and then ringing the defendant's solicitors and my clerks to keep them up to date. It was only much later in the day that I would go into Chambers to pick up any work for the following day. I quite deliberately kept out of the way of the ladies on the top floor. I had visions of them meeting over tea and biscuits to brand me a trouble maker and conniving little bitch. I could hear them in my head saying 'We told you she was bad news.'

I reckoned I was getting the hang of being a barrister and I liked it. But even better than that I was actually not a bad barrister at all. During the months of January and February I was busy doing case after case in the County Court. They were mainly family matters, in particular emergency applications for non-molestation orders and sometimes final hearings for a permanent order. I soon had the procedure off pat and addressed the court like an old hand. On January 21, I was back in my all time favourite court – Number One at Camberwell Magistrates' Court. As I took my seat in counsel's row, I remembered the magistrate telling my stepfather, Eastman, what would happen if he assaulted me again. Eastman was shaking in case the 'judge' sent him to the jailhouse. The magistrate bound him over in his own recognisance of two hundred pounds. Stupid old Eastman thought he had to pay then and there, until the magistrate explained it would be forfeit only if he interfered with me again. Now I half hoped it would be the same magistrate, but it wasn't. My case had been over ten years ago, so he had probably gone into a well-deserved retirement. I also remembered the criticism members of my Chambers had made that I would not be able to find my way to the lesser courts, because I had spent too much time with Mike in Sheffield and the Old Bailey. I was by now more than familiar with the main courts where members of Chambers were briefed. As for the criticism that my voice was too soft and I would never make myself heard in court, especially in cross-examination, well none of the judges had any problem hearing me. The clients did not think I was a softly spoken pushover. I was not a wimp. The clerks would acknowledge that the good name of Tooks Court was safe in my hands.

Towards the end of February I was informed by Helena Kennedy that a Chambers meeting was due to take place in the first week of March to deal with the letter I had sent to Chambers. Was there anything I would like to add to it? I said there was not. She told me that the meeting was to take place on March 2, but contrary to the normal rule at Tooks Court, I would not be allowed to attend, since tenants wanted to feel free to discuss me. No other pupils would attend. That sounded fair to me.

On the March 2, I did not go near Chambers. The following day I did go in, but no one spoke to me. Nor did they for the rest of that week and the following week. I had thought that the whole point of the meeting was to respond to my letter, but it was obvious to me that whatever had taken place, everyone was remaining schtumm. This was bizarre. It was not as if I was being considered for a tenancy. Tooks Court had rejected me and all I wanted was the reason. I was sure, even positive, that Mike Mansfield did not like or approve of what had happened to me. He was embarrassed, that was certainly the impression that I got, otherwise he would have spoken to me.

Eventually Len Woodley came in to see me. He was obviously not in court, because he was wearing a tweed jacket and flannel trousers.

'Hello Constance, get your coat, and let's go and have a cup of tea.'

I followed Len out of Chambers and out on to Chancery Lane.

'It's a crying shame' he said as we walked together. 'I don't know. I voted for that lot having a tenancy and now see how they behave.'

We went to the sandwich bar on the corner of Chancery Lane and High Holborn. He ordered a tea for me and a coffee for himself.

'Have they given you any reasons yet Constance?'

'No, Len.'

'Well that's interesting,' said Len. 'I'd be interested to hear what they have to say, because they don't have any reasons, not really.'

I drank my tea. It was all becoming a bit confusing, I thought.

'I'm not staying here,' said Len.

'I'm sorry,' I said, 'shall we go?'

'No,' said Len. 'I meant I can't stay at Tooks Court, not after that.'

I had no idea what *that* meant and I felt that it was not my place to ask him.

'You've certainly done it this time, Constance, because I can tell you now that a number of people were not happy with what happened in the Chambers' meeting and I would be very surprised if they remain in these Chambers by the end of the week.'

I could not believe my ears. We finished our drink and went back to Chambers and Len disappeared into his room. I went up to the top floor, collected my work and went home. I was troubled by what Len had said. Things were not looking too good.

On April 1, I went into Chambers and there was a white envelope with Janet Plange's handwriting on the front. It was addressed to 'Constance Briscoe' and marked 'private and confidential'. I opened the envelope and pulled out the letter, it was dated 27 March 1986.

Dear Constance

It was decided at a Chambers meeting on March 2, 1986 that you would be given 6 months in which to make arrangements to leave Chambers. We therefore hope you will be ready

to leave on or before September 2, 1986. If you need any
references please do not hesitate to speak to your former pupil
masters or another senior member of Chambers or me about
future prospects.

Your sincerely,
Michael Mansfield
on behalf of Chambers

So they had finally decided to throw me out. That did not come
as a surprise to me at all, since I had not asked Chambers to
reconsider their earlier decision. What I was surprised about
was the fact that I had asked for reasons in my letter of
December 9, 1985 and still I was not given them. I read the
letter again. It was typed, but Mike had hand-written the name
'Constance'. It was definitely his signature and he had added to
the bottom of the typed letter in his own hand the words 'see
me about future prospects'.

I felt like writing another letter, which simply said 'Go to
Hell'.

I was just contemplating that, when Mike walked in.

'Oh, Constance,' he said 'about that letter.'

Mike looked positively uncomfortable in my presence. He
could see me clearly enough looking at the letter.

'So it's curtains, Mike.'

'I'm sorry, Constance,' he said, 'but that is the decision of
Chambers.'

'Well, what does it mean, Mike? Am I going to be thrown
out?'

'No, Constance, you will not be thrown out.'

'Well, what does it mean Mike?'

'It means, Constance, that you should make every effort to
find another set of chambers. If you need more time let me
know.'

'And if I do not find another set by then, Mike, then
what?'

Mike was silent for a while and I was certainly not making things any easier for him. We sat in silence and occasionally Mike's discomfort was broken by his smile. It would have been easier if he wasn't so dishy. Well, I wasn't going to get sidetracked like that.

'When I wrote to Chambers on December 9, I thought that they were going to have a Chambers meeting to give me the reasons for my rejection.' Mike nodded. 'Well, if you read that letter, there are no reasons stated.'

'No reasons?'

'No reasons,' I said, pushing the letter across the table to Mike. 'You have seen that letter Mike because you signed it.'

'Constance, of course, how could we forget.'

'Well, what are the reasons, Mike? Why was I turned down in the first place?'

There was silence.

'Constance,' he said eventually, 'I will see that you are informed of the reasons why you were turned down.'

He put his finger in between his collar and his neck and pulled down on his shirt. He was flushed. 'I will arrange for you to have the reasons by tomorrow. You cannot have a tenancy here, but I would like you to know that I am very supportive and if you need any references please ask me.'

'Thank you Mike,' I said.

I was really not feeling too well and I collected up my things. Outside the wind slapped me in the face and took my breath away and suddenly I felt clear headed again. When I got home, I did not bother to get undressed, I jumped straight into my four-poster bed fully clothed. My future was now blowing in the wind along the draughty roads of Chancery Lane, but I felt safe as long as I was in my bed.

I was woken up with a slap to my face. It rocked my neck. I opened my eyes to get my bearings and to see what had happened. I was running the whole incident through my mind's eye when I felt another slap.

'So you're tired. You want to give up. Go on, give up. See if I care.'

'Oh, Miss K, it's you. Where have you been?'

'Get up, get up. In bed in your suit! Whatever next. Get up this minute.'

'But I'm tired.'

The duvet started to slide down the bed. I got up and got undressed, as Miss K sat at the bottom of my bed with one leg on the bed and the other nowhere to be seen. She fiddled with the neck of her twinset. I got back into bed and started to cry. I had really, really and truly had enough. I was so tired and my face hurt. I fell asleep again and when my alarm went in the morning Miss K was nowhere to be seen.

I did not wish to go to Tooks Court at all, but I did want my reasons. Somehow I forced myself to dress and go down the stairs and out the door. I had a touch of the giddies again and it had not gone away when I took my place at my desk on the top floor. Helena was passing by and popped her head round the door to say she was very sorry about the way it had all ended. I thanked her for her support, but even she repeated the mantra that it had nothing to do with my ability it was simply a question of balance in Chambers. I tried very hard to settle down and get my work done. I forced myself to concentrate.

It was just before one o'clock when Adrian Fulford put his head round the door. He was looking, as ever, absolutely fabulous.

'Fancy a cup of coffee, Constance?'

'No thank you, Adrian', I said, 'I've got quite a bit of work to do.'

'Well, Constance,' said Adrian, 'I've been appointed to give you the reasons why Chambers turned you down. Let us go and get a tea or coffee.'

He had his jacket slung casually over his shoulder, but he put it on and took me to the café at the top of Chancery Lane. I asked for a tea. When we were seated, he did not waste time on small talk.

'Now Constance, I want you to know that I have been appointed as a spokesperson to give you the reasons you were not given a tenancy and you must understand they do not express my views, in fact far from it.' I sipped my tea and waited. 'One day, Constance, you will know the true reasons, but I have been asked to tell you that there is simply a problem of balance in Chambers. That is the official reason.'

'I have been told that already, but you say there are other reasons, real reasons?'

'Yes,' said Adrian. 'I will tell you. They can be summed up in one word: jealousy. Maybe two words: pure jealousy. Some of the women have said that you wear make-up and have straightened your hair, which shows that you have lost your black consciousness, and you are over familiar with white men.'

'What!' I said.

'Yes, Constance.'

'Over familiar with white men?'

'Yes, and I believe you could include Mike Fisher in that group.'

I was stunned and for a minute I was silenced.

'As I say, Constance, it is pure jealousy, but there is some very good news.'

'What is that, Adrian?'

'Although it was thought too late to reconsider your application, the meeting decided that never again could personal reasons be used to prevent a candidate from joining as a tenant.'

'That is good news, Adrian?'

'Yes it is, but I am afraid it does not help you.'

'Why were you asked to give me the reasons, Adrian?'

'Because, Constance, it is a known fact that we get on very well and I regard you as a friend.'

'Well, thank you for giving me the reasons.'

'Constance, I am ashamed and deeply embarrassed, but you will be all right. After all this I'm sure you will be only too glad to be rid of us. You know those amongst us who will give you good references.'

Well, at least I had my reasons now; no one could ever say that I hadn't been told. We finished our drinks and I went back to Chambers. Adrian had a conference to go to.

Sitting in my room it was difficult to imagine the happy times I had experienced when I began my pupillage with Mike and thought all my dreams were coming true. I could not believe I was being thrown out because of remarks about my personal appearance. I truly thought Tooks Court was above all that. I had thought that the only reason for rejection could be lack of ability, but not a bit of it.

18
Life Experience

1987

It was now April and I had to find another home soon, or my dream of becoming a barrister would be over. Adrian Fulford and Helena Kennedy busied themselves helping me find another set of Chambers. Helena could at times barely contain her anger at the way that I had been treated. Adrian said he would have a word with Lord Gifford; he knew him well and had previously been in his Chambers. I was sure Tony would remember me from Orgreave.

I sent my CV to his Chambers in Wellington Street, together with a covering letter explaining why I had not been taken on at Tooks Court and that I thought I could bring my work with me. I got a prompt reply. They had a vacancy and were interviewing though they had lots of applicants. I was given a date and time to attend. It could not come quickly enough.

On the appointed day I got out the shirt I had bought from Betty's and made sure it was crisp and white and smelling of my favourite perfume. My shoes were nicely polished and my skirt was not too short, nor was it too long. I had that fresh breath confidence that is commended in the advertisements for toothpaste. As I put on my make-up, I thought that my experience at Tooks Court had convinced me of one thing – I would wear make-up until I was too old to put it on myself. If others did not like it, they could lump it. I did not look too bad. I no longer thought I was ugly, ugly, ugly, but the scars on my face did not look like they were fading.

Wellington Street is in Covent Garden. The Chambers were

above a restaurant or some such similar outlet rather unusual for a barristers' Chambers. I introduced myself to the receptionist and informed her that I had an appointment. I was shown into a waiting room and offered a cup of tea. I declined as I was a bit nervous about the interview and, knowing myself as I do, I did not want to run out for a pee. After about five or ten minutes the receptionist returned and invited me to follow her. I was led into a large room which faced out onto Wellington Street. The interviewing panel consisted of Lord Gifford, two men and two women. One each of the men and women was black. Although they made me feel most welcome, I had a feeling that this was not going to be my lucky day.

Lord Gifford kicked off by reminding me that we had bumped into one other in Sheffield during the miners' strike. He introduced the others and then asked me to call him Tony. Once that was done, he explained that his Chambers were rather out of the ordinary. In other Chambers each barrister kept his own earnings; here they operated as a co-operative. Each barrister worked as part of a team; no-one worked for themselves; all the income they earned went into a common pot and at the end of every month each barrister was paid an income from the pot. This meant that everyone helped each other and the strongest helped the weakest. There was, he said, an incentive for everyone to work hard and do well because if they did not, it meant that the individual was letting down the rest of the group. I rather preferred the idea of keeping the money I earnt for myself, but I nevertheless expressed my agreement.

I was then asked why it was that Tooks Court had refused to take me on when I had spent so much time there. I said that there was a problem with balance at the lower end of Chambers. Some of the panel laughed. They obviously understood what the phrase meant. 'There is always a problem with balance at the bottom of any Chambers,' one of them said. Then one of the women leant forward.

'What do you think about men who rape women?'

'What do I think?'

'Well, would you represent them?'

I had not really thought about that actually and I was far too junior to be instructed in a rape case. As I was thinking about it, she asked again.

'Would you feel comfortable about representing them?'

'Well, I've never been instructed in a rape case.'

'We have a policy of not representing a defendant charged with rape where the issue is consent,' one of them said.

This was not consistent with the cab-rank rule, whereby barristers are obliged to take on a case, however unpopular the defendant. They were all looking at me to gauge my reaction.

'And I agree with that policy,' I said. I felt a bit like Judas.

'Tell us about you, Constance,' said Lord Gifford. I see from your CV that you have worked as an auxiliary at King's College Hospital, St George's Hospital and at a hospice for the terminally ill. Did you ever consider becoming a doctor?'

'No.'

'But you have extensive experience in that area.'

'Yes, but I never considered going into medicine – it was just a way of earning money. I think if you look on my CV you will see that I have experience working in legal advice centres.'

'I see you worked voluntarily giving advice at Brixton Advice Centre and also at the Brixton Law Community Centre,' said the white female. 'You have been busy.'

'What is it that really gets you going?' asked Lord Gifford. 'What are you really passionate about?'

'I don't know,' I said, 'but if I had to choose, I think I would say injustice.'

'Injustice?' said Lord Gifford. 'What do you mean by that?'

'Well,' I said, 'some people are born into privilege and they will never struggle. For them life is easy. Other people are not that lucky. Through circumstances outside their control, they are born into hardship. Their life is a constant struggle. I do not think that is fair.'

'And where do you place yourself in that example you have given?'

'I have my problems,' I said.

Fortunately they did not press me. When the interview was over, I made my way out onto the street. I was not hopeful. My answers on rape had been too hesitant.

At the end of the week I was surprised to get a call in Tooks Court from Lord Gifford. 'How are you, Constance?' he said.

'I'm fine, thank you.'

There was no hesitation at all.

'I suppose you want to know what we have decided?'

I remained silent.

'Well I'm sorry, we were unable to offer you a place in our Chambers. but I'm sure you will do well wherever you go.'

'Thank you for informing me,' I said.

'Oh please, there is no need for that. I'm just sorry that I am the bearer of bad news.'

'Are there any particular reasons why you felt unable to offer me a tenancy?'

'Well, since you ask we felt that you have commitment and a good practice, but we felt that you lacked experience of life.'

'Experience of life?' I said.

'Yes, you have a certain naive quality about you which we were not sure would go down well with our clients. I am sorry we were unable to offer you a place, but we are sure that you will find a home soon.'

'Oh,' I said. 'Thanks.'

Tony Gifford put the phone down, his duty done. I was not actually that surprised that they had not offered me a place, but to say I lacked experience of life was a bloody cheek!

Back in Chambers we were all informed that there was a demonstration that would take place that weekend to call for the release of Nelson Mandela. It would start in Hyde Park and end up outside the South African Embassy. The anti-apartheid movement was expecting tens of thousands of people. Any left-wing Chambers worth their reputation would be there. We were not exactly given a three line whip, but we were warmly encouraged to make every effort to go. I had nothing to do that weekend, so I decided to go on the march. There were thousands of people there in Hyde Park. The sun was shining and everyone was in a good mood. I was just following the crowd, lost in my own thoughts as I marched towards Trafalgar Square. I had not spotted anyone from Chambers, but then again I was not exactly looking for anyone. We were pretty close to Trafalgar Square when I thought I heard someone call my name.

'Hello, Constance,' I heard. I looked around but I could not see anyone. Then I heard it again. 'Constance, wait.' I turned round, but the crowd was dense and I had no idea whether or not it was my imagination. As I was scanning the crowd someone touched my left elbow. I turned round and saw it was Lord Gifford.

'Hello, Constance,' he said, 'what a wonderful day!'

'Hello, Lord Gifford.'

'Call me, Tony'

'Hello, Tony.'

'What a wonderful day.'

'Yes, it is.'

'Do you mind if I walk with you?'

'No, of course not,' I said as I turned and continued to walk with the crowd.

We walked and talked in the sunshine, about Nelson Mandela, Tony's Chambers, even the beautiful weather. I really did not have a great deal to add to the conversation. I was acutely conscious that the relationship between us was not exactly equal. I was a pupil with nowhere to go and he was a Head of Chambers. Gradually he encouraged me to talk about my work and the people I liked at Tooks Court. Tony knew them all well. We had walked together for about two miles when he bought me an ice cream. I was fantastically hot. I removed my long sleeved shirt and tied it round my waist as we walked. He really was very easy company. For a time we walked in silence, just taking in the sunshine and the atmosphere. He was looking up at the sky when he said:

'I'm really sorry we were not able to help you, but there is always very serious competition for vacancies in Chambers.'

He sounded as if he felt personally bad about it.

'Well, these things happen,' I said.

'Yes, it is a pity that we cannot accommodate all pupils,' he said, still looking at the sky.

We walked some more. I turned sideways to look at him – he was tall, six foot plus and he was not bad looking, I suppose. Maybe a Lord should be tall, but then again I had no idea what a Lord looked like.

'What were the reasons again?' I said.

'What reasons?' said Tony, as if musing.

'The reasons why I was turned down,'

He had to think about it for a moment.

'Well,' Tony said, almost embarrassed, 'the reasons were that you lacked worldly experience.'

'I lack worldly experience?' I said. 'That is a bit rich coming from a Lord.' He was silent for a minute and then he started to laugh.

'Well, yes, I suppose it is.

We walked along in a much lighter mood. He spoke about his children, a boy and a girl, his former wife, Lady Gifford, and his new partner with whom he was very much in love. We stood shoulder to shoulder outside the South African Embassy singing 'Free Nelson Mandela' songs. We went for a cup of tea afterwards and then we parted and went our separate ways.

To my surprise he rang again the next week.

'How about a drink?'

'Sure.'

'Fifteen minutes in Daly's.'

Daly's was a wine bar on the corner of the Strand and Essex Street. We shared a bottle of wine. Tony was in good spirits and spoke non-stop about his politics.

'How are you doing on the pupillage side of things?'

'Not good.'

He offered to help in any way that he could. When I reminded him that he could have helped some time ago by offering me a place in his Chambers, he got embarrassed. He asked what I would do next.

'Oh,' I said, 'I think the first thing I need to do is gain some more wordly experience.'

Tony looked slightly ill at ease but I laughed and he did too and we instantly became comfortable drinking partners again. Tony offered to give me a reference if I needed one. Quite what he could say I don't know because he only knew what I told him and that was not a great deal. He suggested a picnic on the Sunday after the flicks and I agreed.

'Where's your girlfriend?' I asked.

He told me she was abroad, and assured me that he was not intending to cheat on her. We drank up and left.

Back in Chambers there was a note in my pigeon hole.

'Squatters and pupils are reminded that your arrangements to leave Chambers should be complete on or before September 2.'

I was on a countdown to nowhere.

The picnic in Hyde Park was superb. Tony had gone to a lot of trouble – salami, olives, cheese, french bread and wine in plastic glasses. He was a very nice man, committed, passionate, but if anyone was naive it was him, not me.

Although he asked question after question about my life, I told him that I did not discuss it. When he enquired why that was, I said that I had never discussed my life with anyone. The most I would say was that I did not get on with my mother.

The conversation turned back to Tony and his girlfriend. She travelled extensively and completely trusted Tony not to cheat on her, which he assured me he never did. Tony suggested that when she was next in town all three of us should go out for a drink. I said I would look forward to that. We stayed in the park until the sun went down and then we made our way to the underground station. I thanked Tony for a wonderful picnic and he suggested that we do it again soon. I agreed on condition that I saw the contents of his girlfriend's handbag sooner rather than later.

19
The Dinner Party

1986

Ever since I had left university I had spent two hours every Wednesday at the Brixton Advice Centre, situated in the very heart of Brixton. The Advice Centre had advertised for more lawyers and I had responded to the ad. There I, together with other lawyers, would give my time and free legal advice to those who could not afford it. There were quite a few of us, mainly solicitors from the big firms in the City of London, who had a social conscience. Working on my shift was a commercial lawyer called Adam. I had not really come across him before, but during my holiday I spent more time at the Advice Centre and got to know him. He was obviously very clever. I found him very sympathetic to my views.

Eventually he invited me to a dinner party at his Docklands flat. He told me he had invited five other guests.

Adam was tall, about six foot, with dark hair, well cut in a city slick, parted on the side and neatly layered. His manners were impeccable. He usually wore a very smart suit – thick dark grey material, trousers with turn-ups and three pleats in the front waistband. It was not the type of suit that you could buy now, because that design no longer existed. It was probably made during the Great Gatsby period, but I liked its old-fashioned look.

'Nice suit,' I said as I passed him on the stairs.

'Do you like it? It used to belong to my father.'

'I knew it.'

'Sorry?'

'Nothing,' I said.
'Will we see you on Saturday?'
'Yes, definitely.'
'Seven for seven-thirty.'
'See you then,' I said.

From the station I had to walk for twenty five minutes to Adam's flat – it was a good thing I was not wearing high heels with my mustard yellow top and black mid-length skirt. His flat was on the ground floor of a very modern building; there was a speaker by the main door and you had to ring the bell and then identify yourself, before the door opened automatically. Adam opened the door to his flat wearing a large blue apron.

'Hello, Constance,' he said. 'Good to see you!'

'Hello, Adam,' I replied and handed him a bottle of wine which I had picked up from Sainsbury's. I did not know much about wine, so I hoped he liked it. Two couples were already there and they got up to greet me. We shook hands while Adam went off to get me a drink. I knew Andrew and Martin from the Advice Centre, but I did not know their girlfriends.

The men seemed to know one another from way back. They had been at school together and then at either Oxford or Cambridge University. Some had read Law and others subjects like Classics. I had found them a good bunch to work with and they all had a strong social conscience. I got the impression that this was not the first dinner party they had been to at Adam's. Andrew asked Adam if he would be cooking one of his complicated recipes at which all present laughed. 'Seven for eight-fifteen,' one of the others said. There was more laughter. Maybe Adam was a good cook, maybe he was a slow cook. The worst situation would be if he was a slow bad cook, but that was unlikely, or no one would go come to his dinner parties. I took a peek into the kitchen. I could see what Andrew meant by seven for eight-fifteen. Adam had food piled all over the place, Bottles of alcohol lined up in rows of red followed by white, followed by sparkling water, followed by still. There was a plate just with fancy bread rolls with seeds on the top. Adam appeared to be in the thick of it with his sleeves rolled up.

'You all right there Adam?' I said. 'Do you want a hand?'

'No, he does not want a hand, Constance,' said Andrew. 'He is perfectly happy.'

'Come and join us. If he needs help, it will be a first.'

The only time Adam came out was when the intercom buzzer went. He rushed to the front door and introduced us to Don, a friend from law school. Don did not wait to be offered a drink, but he asked Adam for a large red. We were all informed that the first course would be served in ten minutes. That was the last time the group saw Adam for quite some time. He went back to keep the meat under control. The poor boy looked flustered. He had flour in his hair, streaks of what looked like strawberry down the side of his face and his apron now looked like an artist's palette. Twenty minutes later, at about 8.15, Adam invited us to take our place at the table. I was placed next to him with Andrew on my right. Adam had set the table out immaculately. Our first course was salmon wrapped in vine leaves, then steak with a pepper sauce, sauté potatoes, mange-tout, baby carrots and spinach. He had gone to a lot of trouble. The men wolfed down the steak and asked for seconds. Adam had bought loads too much. The girls took their time with their steak, it was delicious. I was tempted to ask for more, but I decided I had better stick with the girls on this one. There was much silly talk around the dinner table and the impression I got was that none of the girls were part of a couple, although they were hoping to be by the end of the evening. Dan gave the impression he did not care whether he was a couple or not as long as the alcohol continued to flow. I wondered if Adam had a girlfriend. Presumably not as he had invited me.

I helped him to clear the second course, while Dan poured

more wine into the glasses. We had to wait for an eternity for the next dish which Adam said was called crème brulée, cream with burnt sugar on top. He had an individual crème brulée for each of us. No one complained about the wait, there was enough wine and talk to keep us going. I drank mainly water, but the others were getting quite merry. All the men were solicitors in large City firms working for megabucks clients. I was nowhere close. When I told them I did crime they asked what sort, but that was very difficult to describe because the only real work I had been involved in was the miners' strike. They seemed quite impressed by that. I told them about Tooks Court and that my pupil master was Mike Mansfield. They all seemed to know who he was, which surprised me. Commercial lawyers do not keep up to date with radical lawyers

'Isn't he that left wing lawyer who's always on the telly?' asked one of the girls.

'Are you staying on at Tooks Court?' asked Andrew.

'Probably not. I'd like some wider experience.'

'Where are thinking of applying?'

'I'm not sure at the moment.'

Fortunately the quality of the dessert diverted them from my career or lack of it. I was extremely surprised that Adam could cook so well. The meal concluded with cheese, port and coffee. Adam had been to Oxford. He had studied languages and had wanted to become an immigration lawyer, but ended up in the City doing big deals. His brothers had also studied at Oxford and Cambridge. His father was a surgeon and his mother was a paediatrician. I warmed to him; he had real class and when he asked me if I would like to go out some time, I agreed. It must have been close to midnight when his guests started looking at their watches. I was keen to get back home, but I offered to tidy up first. There was really no need to do that, Adam said, but he was very glad when I did. Adam made some coffee for us and Dan drove me to the station. I had agreed with Adam that we would talk next at the Advice Centre on Wednesday. It was a good night. I liked the company of clever men.

The following weekend I went out with Adam. He had impeccable manners, which I attributed to his public school education. In any event I must have passed the test because he wanted to see me again mid-week. This time we went for a walk around the streets of Brixton. On our third date we went for a meal and he stayed overnight at my house. He was a passionate man.

Back at Tooks Court I sent out five letters every week and kept a running response/action diary. By the time we got to September I was more than desperate but on September 9 I received some good news. Waiting for me in my pigeon hole were two letters. The first was from 2 Garden Court, Middle Temple.

> Dear Ms Briscoe,
>
> Thank you for your application for a tenancy in these Chambers. You have been shortlisted and I should therefore be grateful if you would attend here for an interview at 6.15 pm next Thursday.
>
> Please let me know as soon as possible whether this is convenient.
>
> Best wishes
> Courtney Griffiths

The second letter was from 4 Brick Court:

> Dear Constance Briscoe,
>
> Thank you for your letter enquiring about a tenancy. Would you please telephone the clerk to Chambers in order to arrange a meeting between yourself and Andrew Bano who is our Head of Chambers.
>
> Yours faithfully
> Tony Wadling

I rang both Chambers immediately and confirmed interview dates. Back home I tried on a number of suits for my interview.

I wanted to look good. Betty's suits from Camberwell Green came to my rescue. I had at least half a dozen suits from her, but for some reason I could not get the first skirt over my hips. I tried the second suit, but had the same problem. I was not conscious of over-eating. OK, I had been eating posh cheese and olives, but that could not explain my bulging hips. I stood on the scales. I was a good stone over my regular weight. I almost passed out – literally, I had a dizzy fit. I made an appointment the next day to go and see the doctor. Waiting in the holding area I was trying to work out where and when I had been over-eating. I definitely was bigger and my bottom wobbled when I walked. I explained to the doctor my weight gain and he examined me and took blood and urine samples. I agreed to call him in seven days' time.

The following day I had an appointment for a massage. I removed my clothes but kept my knickers on. The therapist was very good and whilst I did not go in for all that fancy nonsense, she used her oils on my back, legs, arms and stomach and when she got to my lower abdomen she said 'What's this, Constance?'

'What's what?' I said.

'This lump.'

I had no idea what she was on about. She tapped on my stomach twice.

'Constance,' she said, 'you are pregnant.'

I almost fell off the massage table. I could not be. I was a good Catholic girl. God would never forgive me. We had followed the teachings of the Catholic faith and not used a condom. Now according to this lady, I was pregnant. Did she really know? Seven days later my doctor confirmed it. That was all I needed. Adam knew nothing about it and I had no intention of telling him for now. We had never talked about children and I had no idea how he would react. This was my problem.

The following Thursday I attended an interview at Garden

Court. I thought that it was obvious that I was pregnant. My belly walked before me. I was led into an interview room where four members of Chambers were waiting for me. The only one I can now remember is Courtney Griffiths, who introduced everyone to me. About seven minutes into the interview Courtney said

'We are very impressed by your references Constance, but tell me is there any one else at Christian Fisher who could have provided you with a reference apart from Mike Fisher?

I was taken aback for a moment, but the significance of his question was not lost on me. Of course rumour had it that Mike Fisher and I were an item, that had been one of the reasons for my not getting the tenancy at Tooks Court which was entirely erroneous, but Courtney Griffiths did not know that. He had assumed that Mike Fisher had provided me with a reference because he was my sleeping partner, bloody cheek. While the others waited for a reply I calmed my nerves and toned down my response.

'Mike Fisher is the senior partner at the firm,' I said. 'I had not considered getting references from other solicitors at the practice because I had assumed that a reference from the senior partner would be sufficient. If you want other references from other solicitors at the practice, I could obtain them if I was given details of who exactly were required to give references.'

Courtney did not pursue the point, but moved on to another topic. It was really all a waste of time. I knew that there was no way in a month of Sundays that he would support my application. The farce continued for twenty minutes and by the time he asked me whether there was anything else I wanted to say, I felt sick. I said a polite, 'No, thank you,' though all I wanted to say, was 'Sod off, Courtney Griffiths.' He thanked me for coming. I thanked him for inviting me to the interview and I was shown out. I paused for breath at Fountain Court. That interview had not gone very well. Walking back to Tooks Court I walked past 4 Brick Court, which was on my left as I made my way to

Chancery Lane. I could only hope that I had better luck with them.

I knew before I got the letter from Garden Court that it would tell me to get lost. It was short and to the point. They were unable to offer me a place in their Chambers. Competition, as I would know, was stiff and unfortunately everyone could not be offered a tenancy. I was not going to lose any sleep over them. Tony Gifford was very kind. He rang me several times during the week and gave me a lot of sensible advice. He really was a very good friend.

I had left a brief message at 4 Brick Court and I was invited to attend an interview the following week. When the day came, I put on my make-up, combed my hair and walked down Chancery Lane to Brick Court. I have to say I had no real enthusiasm for this interview; after so many disappointments I felt that I was being invited so they could turn me down. I introduced myself to the receptionist and was invited to wait in the waiting room. It was very nice, very low key. I hardly knew anyone at the Chambers. When I was ushered into the interview room everyone stood up and introduced themselves to me which was quite different from the other interviews I had attended. They asked very general questions about my work and what percentage of my work was Family.

'It is not the main part of my practice, but I hope to build on it,' I said.

'Do you enjoy Family law?'

'Yes I do. I find it challenging, but rewarding to deal with the clients. I still want to continue doing some crime.'

'How soon are you expected to leave Tooks Court?'

'By the end of the year.'

The interview ended and they all thanked me for coming and again stood up when I left the room. What nice people! It was a good interview. I did not feel stressed at all and the panel was extremely friendly and concerned about my predicament with Tooks Court. You can imagine my surprise when I received a letter dated October 29,1986 from Tony Wadling on behalf of the pupillage committee.

> Dear Constance Briscoe,
>
> Thank you for coming for the interview in Chambers regarding your application for a pupillage. I am sorry that I have not written before now but we have been considering whether we would be able to consider you for a tenancy with us in the next twelve months. I am afraid that we have concluded that we cannot and it would not therefore be fair to you to make any offer of pupillage.
>
> However, if you are required to leave Tooks Court at the end of this year and you need somewhere from which to continue making applications for a tenancy, please contact us and we will do our best to help you.
>
> Yours faithfully
>
> Tony Wadling
>
> Pupillage Secretary

I had been thrown a temporary lifeline. Brick Court was the first and only Chambers to offer such a lifeline. I had less than two months to go and the most I had managed to secure was a lifeline! I went off to find Michael Mansfield in his room.

'Mike,' I said, 'can I have a word?'

'Sure, Constance, come in.'

I entered and sat at the desk in the chair that I had sat in when I was first his pupil. If only I had known then what I knew now, I might not have sat so comfortably.

'Can I help, Constance?'

Mike looked tired, but he was still good looking and he had eyes like Father Battle's.

'Is there any chance, Mike, that I will be allowed to stay on beyond December?'

Mike thought about it for a moment.

'I very much doubt it, Constance, but I can ask if you like. From your point of view, if there is no realistic prospect of you being taken on here, then there is a good argument for saying that the sooner you start again elsewhere the better.'

Mike was right, of course, and I really did not wish to stay at Tooks Court. The writing was on the wall.

'Anything else?' Mike asked.

'No.'

'How are you getting on?'

'Not good, Mike.'

'Well, if there is anything you want me to do, just say.'

I thanked Mike and left the room. I had almost exhausted the list of Chambers that I had first targeted. My rejection pile was full of 'no vacancies, but we do wish you luck' letters. For the whole of November I kept my ear to the ground, but I heard nothing about vacancies in other sets, nothing, absolutely nothing. On Tony Gifford's advice, I wrote to 4 Brick Court:

> Dear Tony Wadling,
>
> Thank you for your letter of October 28. At our last informal interview you will recall that I mentioned that I would be required to leave Tooks Court on December 31, 1986.
>
> Having considered the position and the very kind invitation that was extended to me in your last letter I would very much like to join your chambers for a period of six months so that I can continue to apply to other Chambers.
>
> I therefore now write to ask whether it might be possible for me to join you from January 1 to July 31, 1987
>
> I look forward to hearing from you at your earliest convenience.
>
> Constance Briscoe

I heard nothing for a couple of weeks. Whilst time was running out, I was past caring. I was pregnant, fed up and required to leave Tooks Court on December 23. I went to Harringey Magistrates' Court. Good old Gracia Stephenson had instructed me in a bail application. When I saw the defendant in the cells, he told me he was desperate for bail. This was effectively the last chance that he would have to get out of jail before the festive shutdown. If he failed, there would be no celebratory festive dip in Trafalgar Square fountain on New Year's Eve for him. I have absolutely no idea what it was that swayed the magistrates, but they granted bail on stringent conditions. He had to be indoors by 10 pm even on Christmas Eve and New Year's Eve. He was not happy at all, but it was better than staying in jail over the shutdown. Gracia was pleased when I rang in to report the results.

On December 22 I returned from Horseferry Magistrates' Court early in the morning and there was a message for me in the pigeon hole to call Mr. Wadling. I went to my room and called the number I had. Mr Wadling was pleased to inform me that Chambers was prepared to agree to my request and their clerks would expect me to start at Brick Court in the New Year. If I wanted to, I could move all my papers over before the Christmas shutdown. I thanked Mr. Wadling and informed him I would move my papers the next day.

On December 23 I returned from Thames Magistrates' Court to Tooks Court. As I checked my briefs I isolated those which were mine and rang each solicitor to ask whether they wished me to continue to be instructed in the case or whether they were happy with the brief staying at Tooks Court. Once that was done I collected the relevant briefs and walked over to Brick Court. There was already a pigeon hole there for me with my name on it. I introduced myself to the clerks, placed my briefs in the in-tray and walked back to Tooks Court. I checked once more that I had not left anything behind. Removing my key from my key ring, I handed it to the senior clerk and made my way down the stairs and out of the front door. I was done for at Tooks Court.

Epilogue

My son was born on June 24, 1987. I was offered a permanent tenancy at 4 Brick Court later in 1987. My daughter was born on 23 September, 1989. Adam and I lived together from 1987 to 1999.

I developed a practice mainly in criminal law. In 1994 I became a President of Mental Health Review Tribunals, which reach decisions on whether patients who have had mental disorders are fit to be discharged from hospital. In 1996 I was appointed a part time judge (Assistant Recorder) in the Crown Court. I remained at 4 Brick Court until 1999, when a decision was taken that it should become a specialist family set. I then moved to a leading criminal set. I now have a varied practice including cases of murder, rape and some child abuse.

If you have been affected by any of the issues in **BEYOND UGLY**, *you may find the following helpful. However, the Publisher is not responsible for the contents of those websites.*

....

- **Barnardo's**
  Website: www.barnardos.org.uk

- **BAWSO**
  (Black Association of Women Step Out)
  24 hour helpline: 0800 731 8147
  Website: www.bawso.org.uk

- **Black Women's Mental Health Project**
  Tel: 020 8961 6324
  Website: www.bwmhp.org.uk

- **Childline**
  24 hour helpline: 0800 1111
  Website: www.Childline.org.uk

- **ERIC**
  (Education and Resources for Improving Childhood Continence) is a UK charity that provides information and resources for children, parents and professionals on bed-wetting and other childhood continence problems.
  Helpline: 0845 370 8008
  (weekdays 10–4)
  Website: www.eric.org.uk

- **The Hideout**
  Website: www.thehideout.org.uk

- **Kidscape**
  24 hour helpline: 08451 205 204
  This is for the use of parents, guardians or concerned relatives and friends of bullied children. Children experiencing bullying problems should ring Childline (see above).
  Website: www.kidscape.org.uk

- **NSPCC**
  (National Society for the Prevention of Cruelty to Children)
  24 hour helpline: 0808 800 5000
  Textphone: 0800 056 0566
  Website: www.nspcc.org.uk

- **Refuge**
  24 hour helpline: 0808 2000 247
  Website: www.refuge.org.uk

- **Shakti Women's Aid**
  Tel: 0131 475 2399 (weekdays 9–5. Answering machine service.)
  Website: www.shaktiedinburgh.co.uk

- **Southhall Black Sisters**
  Tel: 020 8571 9595 (weekdays 10–5. Answering machine service.)
  Website: www.southallblacksisters.org.uk